S0-ARM-568

VITAL
IDEAS
SEX

Other books in the VITAL IDEAS series:

VITAL IDEAS: Crime
Edited by Theresa Starkey

VITAL IDEAS: Money
Edited by Dana Heller and Claire Pamplin

VITAL IDEAS: Work
Edited by Christina Boufis

Series Editor: Daniel Born, academic department chair in Kaplan University's legal studies department and lecturer in the MA literature program at Northwestern University's School of Continuing Studies

Volume Editor: Regina Barreca, professor of English at the University of Connecticut

Contributors

Kristine Bergman
Nancy Carr
Steven Craig
Patrick Hurley
Mary Klein
Dylan Nelson
Amy Schuler
Donald H. Whitfield
Mary Williams

Edited by Regina Barreca

THE GREAT BOOKS FOUNDATION
A nonprofit educational organization

Published and distributed by

THE GREAT BOOKS FOUNDATION
A nonprofit educational organization

35 E. Wacker Drive, Suite 400
Chicago, Illinois 60601
www.greatbooks.org

ISBN 978-1-933147-81-9

First printing
9 8 7 6 5 4 3 2 1

Library of Congress Cataloging-in-Publication Data

Vital ideas : sex / edited by Regina Barreca.
p. cm.
ISBN 978-1-933147-81-9 (alk. paper)
1. Sex. 2. Inquiry-based learning. I. Barreca, Regina. II. Title: Sex.
HQ23.V58 2011
306.7--dc23

2011028115

Book cover and interior design: THINK Book Works

About the Great Books Foundation

The Great Books Foundation, publisher of the Vital Ideas series, was established in 1947 by University of Chicago educators Robert Maynard Hutchins and Mortimer Adler. The Foundation is an independent, nonprofit educational organization whose mission is to empower readers of all ages to become more reflective and responsible thinkers. To this end, the Foundation publishes enduring works across the disciplines and conducts workshops in Shared Inquiry,™ a text-based, Socratic method of learning.

Footnotes by an author are not bracketed; footnotes by the Great Books Foundation, an editor, or a translator are [bracketed].

Spelling and punctuation have been modernized and slightly altered for clarity.

Contents

Preface

The idea of sex captures our intellectual imagination as fully as sexual desire captures our physical selves. Since the first pornographers represented human figures engaged in sex acts by scratching pictures on cave walls, we have been driven to express our thoughts about sex in order to puzzle out its meanings. Guided by our own strong appetites and passions, even when those are misguided, we are rarely encouraged to treat the matter of sex candidly and with reasoned perspective. Even in our enlightened age, sex is handled with oohs and ahhs, or giggles and snorts, as if the lover is a magician or a maker of balloon animals. In this volume of the Vital Ideas series, selections range from biblical narrative to the work of Freud to contemporary fiction and academic explorations as we hear the perspectives of those who have dared to *think* about sex rather than chortle or blush.

The Vital Ideas series takes a content-based rather than skills-based approach to reading and composition. It is based on the conviction, supported by the editors' own classroom experience, that students are most motivated to improve their reading and writing skills when they are engaged with subject matter that is meaningful to them. The contents of each volume represent outstanding examples of well-reasoned thought and high-quality writing across a variety of genres. In keeping with the tradition of the Great Books Foundation, the Vital Ideas series is first and foremost designed to stimulate rewarding Shared Inquiry discussions and instill the habits of reflective, critical thinking.

Using the Questions

Each of the selections in this volume is followed by two sets of questions that will help enrich the reader's engagement with what the author has to say.

The "For Discussion" questions ask about the meaning of what the author says, often referring to a specific phrase or passage in the selection. These questions ask readers to form interpretations of the text and are particularly helpful for initiating classroom discussion. They are closely connected with the practice of Shared Inquiry discussion, described at the back of this volume in the "About Shared Inquiry" section.

The questions designated "For Further Reflection" generally ask for a broader response to the selection. These questions work well in conjunction with the "For Discussion" questions but can also be used as prompts for writing assignments, since they encourage not only interpretations of the text, but also the evaluation of its ideas.

In addition, at the back of the book is a set of "Comparison Questions." These questions encourage discussion and writing about issues that are common to two or more selections in the book. Unlike the generic "compare and contrast" questions in many textbooks, the "Comparison Questions" ask readers to critically address specific ideas and points of view that the authors have expressed.

This excerpt from 2 Samuel features King David, well known for his defeat of Goliath, the warrior giant. After David's victory in 1 Samuel, his public stature is greater than that of Saul, the reigning king of Israel, and Saul jealously forces David into exile among Israel's enemies, the Philistines. When Israel and the Philistines fight, Saul recognizes the hopelessness of his situation and takes his own life. Israel loses the battle, and David becomes king of Israel. The events of David's reign, which spanned about fifty years, are recounted in 2 Samuel. Throughout the ages, artists have been drawn to David as a subject—representing the range of virtues and vices of powerful leaders. The text reprinted here is from the New Revised Standard Version of the Bible, which most biblical scholars and linguists regard as the best English translation of the ancient Hebrew.

David and Bathsheba

11 In the spring of the year, the time when kings go
out to battle, David sent Joab with his officers and
all Israel with him; they ravaged the Ammonites, and
besieged Rabbah. But David remained at Jerusalem.
2 It happened, late one afternoon, when David rose
from his couch and was walking about on the roof of
the king's house, that he saw from the roof a woman
bathing; the woman was very beautiful. 3 David sent
someone to inquire about the woman. It was reported,
"This is Bathsheba, daughter of Eliam, the wife of Uriah
the Hittite." 4 So David sent messengers to get her, and
she came to him, and he lay with her. (Now she was
purifying herself after her period.) Then she returned to
her house. 5 The woman conceived; and she sent and told
David, "I am pregnant."

6 So David sent word to Joab, "Send me Uriah the
Hittite." And Joab sent Uriah to David. 7 When Uriah
came to him, David asked how Joab and the people
fared, and how the war was going. 8 Then David said to
Uriah, "Go down to your house, and wash your feet."
Uriah went out of the king's house, and there followed
him a present from the king. 9 But Uriah slept at the
entrance of the king's house with all the servants of his
lord, and did not go down to his house. 10 When they told
David, "Uriah did not go down to his house," David said
to Uriah, "You have just come from a journey. Why did
you not go down to your house?" 11 Uriah said to David,
"The ark and Israel and Judah remain in booths; and

my lord Joab and the servants of my lord are camping
in the open field; shall I then go to my house, to eat and
to drink, and to lie with my wife? As you live, and as
your soul lives, I will not do such a thing." 12Then David
said to Uriah, "Remain here today also, and tomorrow
I will send you back." So Uriah remained in Jerusalem
that day. On the next day, 13David invited him to eat
and drink in his presence and made him drunk; and in
the evening he went out to lie on his couch with the
servants of his lord, but he did not go down to his house.

14In the morning David wrote a letter to Joab, and
sent it by the hand of Uriah. 15In the letter he wrote, "Set
Uriah in the forefront of the hardest fighting, and then
draw back from him, so that he may be struck down and
die." 16As Joab was besieging the city, he assigned Uriah
to the place where he knew there were valiant warriors.
17The men of the city came out and fought with Joab;
and some of the servants of David among the people fell.
Uriah the Hittite was killed as well. 18Then Joab sent
and told David all the news about the fighting; 19and
he instructed the messenger, "When you have finished
telling the king all the news about the fighting, 20then, if
the king's anger rises, and if he says to you, 'Why did you
go so near the city to fight? Did you not know that they
would shoot from the wall? 21Who killed Abimelech son
of Jerubbaal? Did not a woman throw an upper millstone
on him from the wall, so that he died at Thebez? Why
did you go so near the wall?' then you shall say, 'Your
servant Uriah the Hittite is dead too.' "

22So the messenger went, and came and told David
all that Joab had sent him to tell. 23The messenger said
to David, "The men gained an advantage over us, and
came out against us in the field; but we drove them back
to the entrance of the gate. 24Then the archers shot at
your servants from the wall; some of the king's servants

are dead; and your servant Uriah the Hittite is dead also.” 25David said to the messenger, “Thus you shall say to Joab, ‘Do not let this matter trouble you, for the sword devours now one and now another; press your attack on the city, and overthrow it.’ And encourage him.”

26When the wife of Uriah heard that her husband was dead, she made lamentation for him. 27When the mourning was over, David sent and brought her to his house, and she became his wife, and bore him a son.

12 But the thing that David had done displeased the LORD, 1and the LORD sent Nathan to David. He came to him, and said to him, “There were two men in a certain city, the one rich and the other poor. 2The rich man had very many flocks and herds; 3but the poor man had nothing but one little ewe lamb, which he had bought. He brought it up, and it grew up with him and with his children; it used to eat of his meager fare, and drink from his cup, and lie in his bosom, and it was like a daughter to him. 4Now there came a traveler to the rich man, and he was loath to take one of his own flock or herd to prepare for the wayfarer who had come to him, but he took the poor man’s lamb, and prepared that for the guest who had come to him.” 5Then David’s anger was greatly kindled against the man. He said to Nathan, “As the LORD lives, the man who has done this deserves to die; 6he shall restore the lamb fourfold, because he did this thing, and because he had no pity.”

7Nathan said to David, “You are the man!”

FOR DISCUSSION

1. Why does Bathsheba let David know that she is pregnant?
2. Why does David take such elaborate measures to conceal his fatherhood of the child?
3. Why does Uriah refuse to sleep with his wife when he returns from battle?
4. How does Nathan's story of the two men and the lamb relate to the actions of David and Bathsheba?

FOR FURTHER REFLECTION

1. When should the private sexual activities of a political leader become a public matter?
2. Does Bathsheba bear responsibility for the death of her husband?

John Donne (1572–1631) was born in London to a wealthy Roman Catholic family and studied at the University of Oxford and the University of Cambridge, but never received his degree. Donne began working as a secretary for Thomas Egerton, Lord Keeper of the Great Seal, but he lost his job after falling in love with Egerton's niece, Anne More. Her father did not approve of their marriage, and, as a result, Donne and his family lived in poverty for years, during which Donne studied for and eventually became ordained as an Anglican minister. After the death of his wife in 1617, Donne devoted himself to religious duties and quickly became famous as one of the most eloquent preachers in London. His published sermons make up a large portion of his body of literary work. Most of Donne's poetry, however, was not published and recognized until after his death.

To His Mistress Going to Bed

Come, madam, come, all rest my powers defy,
Until I labour, I in labour lie.
The foe oft-times having the foe in sight,
Is tired with standing though he never fight.
Off with that girdle, like heaven's zone glistering,
But a far fairer world encompassing.
Unpin that spangled breastplate which you wear,
That the eyes of busy fools may be stopped there.
Unlace yourself, for that harmonious chime
Tells me from you that now 'tis your bed time.
Off with that happy busk, which I envy,
That still can be, and still can stand so nigh.
Your gown, going off, such beauteous state reveals,
As when from flowry meads the hill's shadow steals.
Off with that wiry coronet and show
The hairy diadem which on you doth grow:
Now off with those shoes, and then safely tread
In this love's hallowed temple, this soft bed.
In such white robes, heaven's angels used to be
Received by men; thou, Angel, bring'st with thee
A heaven like Mahomet's Paradise; and though
Ill spirits walk in white, we easily know
By this these angels from an evil sprite:
Those set our hairs, but these our flesh upright.
   Licence my roving hands, and let them go
Before, behind, between, above, below.
O my America! my new-found-land,
My kingdom, safeliest when with one man manned,

My mine of precious stones, my empery,
How blest am I in this discovering thee!
To enter in these bonds is to be free;
Then where my hand is set, my seal shall be.
    Full nakedness! All joys are due to thee,
As souls unbodied, bodies unclothed must be
To taste whole joys. Gems which you women use
Are like Atlanta's balls, cast in men's views,
That when a fool's eye lighteth on a gem,
His earthly soul may covet theirs, not them.
Like pictures, or like books' gay coverings made
For lay-men, are all women thus arrayed;
Themselves are mystic books, which only we
(Whom their imputed grace will dignify)
Must see revealed. Then, since that I may know,
As liberally as to a midwife, show
Thyself: cast all, yea, this white linen hence,
Here is no penance, much less innocence.
    To teach thee, I am naked first; why then,
What needst thou have more covering than a man.

FOR DISCUSSION

1. What is revealed about the speaker's understanding of his relationship to his mistress in the lines, "O my America! my new-found-land, / My kingdom, safeliest when with one man manned"? (11)
2. Why does the speaker refer to women as "mystic books"? (12)
3. What does the speaker mean in saying, "Here is no penance, much less innocence"? (12)
4. Why does the speaker wait until the very end of the poem to reveal his nakedness?

FOR FURTHER REFLECTION

1. Why doesn't Donne have the woman speak in the poem? If she did, what would she say?
2. Are there reasons why a woman might want to have "more covering than a man"? (12)

Andrew Marvell (1621–1678) was born in Yorkshire, England, and attended Hull Grammar School and Trinity College, Cambridge, from which he received his BA. Little is known about his life immediately following his schooling, except that from 1642 until 1646 he traveled abroad extensively in France, Holland, Switzerland, Spain, and Italy. He is believed to have written most of his best poems around 1650. In 1653 Marvell befriended the poet John Milton, and he was appointed as Milton's assistant during Milton's term as Latin Secretary for the Commonwealth. Marvell continued his involvement in politics, representing Hull in Parliament from 1659 until his death in 1678. Today, he is known as one of the greatest poets of the seventeenth century.

To His Coy Mistress

Had we but world enough, and time,
This coyness, lady, were no crime.
We would sit down, and think which way
To walk, and pass our long love's day.
Thou by the Indian Ganges' side
Shouldst rubies find; I by the tide
Of Humber would complain. I would
Love you ten years before the Flood,
And you should, if you please, refuse
Till the conversion of the Jews.
My vegetable love should grow
Vaster than empires, and more slow;
An hundred years should go to praise
Thine eyes, and on thy forehead gaze;
Two hundred to adore each breast,
But thirty thousand to the rest:
An age at least to every part,
And the last age should show your heart.
For, lady, you deserve this state,
Nor would I love at lower rate.
    But at my back I always hear
Time's wingèd chariot hurrying near;
And yonder all before us lie
Deserts of vast eternity.
Thy beauty shall no more be found,
Nor, in thy marble vault, shall sound
My echoing song; then worms shall try
That long-preserved virginity,

And your quaint honour turn to dust,
And into ashes all my lust:
The grave's a fine and private place,
But none, I think, do there embrace.
    Now therefore, while the youthful hue
Sits on thy skin like morning dew,
And while thy willing soul transpires
At every pore with instant fires,
Now let us sport us while we may,
And now, like amorous birds of prey,
Rather at once our time devour
Than languish in his slow-chapped power.
Let us roll all our strength and all
Our sweetness up into one ball,
And tear our pleasures with rough strife
Thorough the iron gates of life:
Thus, though we cannot make our sun
Stand still, yet we will make him run.

FOR DISCUSSION

1. Why does the speaker call his mistress's resistance to lovemaking a "crime"? (15)
2. Why does the speaker describe in detail how he would woo his mistress if they had infinite time and tell her that "you deserve this state"? (15)
3. Why does the speaker describe the grave where "worms shall try / That long-preserved virginity"? (15)
4. Why does the speaker describe tearing pleasures "with rough strife / Thorough the iron gates of life"? How will taking this pleasure enable the lovers to make "our sun" run? (16)

FOR FURTHER REFLECTION

1. If a prospective lover addressed you as the speaker in this poem does, would that person convince you to cease being coy?
2. Do the threats of death and decay in the poem make the lover's appeal more powerful, or do they undermine it?

Sigmund Freud (1856–1939) was born in Moravia (now the Czech Republic) and grew up in Vienna. He was educated in modern and classical languages and later studied medicine at the University of Vienna. He spent numerous years studying and conducting research in neurology before setting up a practice in neuropsychiatry. At the time, many in the medical community attributed human behavior solely to chemical and physiological causes, but Freud's practice led him to develop the process of psychoanalysis and to delve into the purely psychological causes of behavior. His major publications include *The Interpretation of Dreams* (1900), *Three Essays on the Theory of Sexuality* (1905), *The Ego and the Id* (1923), and *Civilization and Its Discontents* (1930). After the Nazi occupation of Austria in 1938, Freud left for England. He died in London shortly thereafter.

Degradation in Erotic Life

1

If a practicing psychoanalyst asks himself what disorder he is most often called upon to remedy, he is obliged to reply—apart from anxiety in all its many forms—psychical impotence. This strange disorder affects men of a strongly libidinous nature, and is manifested by a refusal on the part of the sexual organs to execute the sexual act, although both before and after the attempt they can show themselves intact and competent to do so, and although a strong mental inclination to carry out the act is present. The man gets his first inkling in the direction of understanding his condition by discovering that he fails in this way only with certain women, whereas it never happens with others. He knows then that the inhibition of his masculine potency is due to some quality in the sexual object, and sometimes he describes having had a sensation of holding back, of having perceived some check within him that interfered successfully with his conscious intention. What this inner opposition is, however, he cannot guess, or what quality in the sexual object makes it active. If the failure has been repeated several times he probably concludes, by the familiar erroneous line of argument, that a recollection of the first occasion acted as a disturbance by causing anxiety and brought about the subsequent failures; the first occasion itself he attributes to some "accidental" occurrence.

Psychoanalytic studies of psychical impotence have already been carried out and published by various writers. Every analyst can, from his own experience, confirm the explanations adduced in them. The disorder is in fact due to the inhibiting influence of certain complexes in the mind that are withdrawn from the knowledge of the person in question. As the most universal feature of this pathogenic materials an incestuous fixation on mother and sister that has not been surmounted stands out. In addition to this, the influence of accidental impressions of a painful kind connected with infantile sexuality comes into consideration, together with those factors that in general reduce the amount of libido available for the female sexual object.

When cases of severe psychical impotence are subjected to exhaustive study by means of psychoanalysis, the following psychosexual processes are found to be operative. Here again—as very probably in all neurotic disorders—the root of the trouble lies in an arrest occurring during the course of development of the libido to that ultimate form that may be called normal. To ensure a fully normal attitude in love, two currents of feeling have to unite—we may describe them as the tender, affectionate feelings and the sensual feelings—and this confluence of the two currents has in these cases not been achieved.

Of these two currents affection is the older. It springs from the very earliest years of childhood, and was formed on the foundation provided by the interests of the self-preservative instinct; it is directed towards the members of the family and those who have care of the child. From the very beginning, elements from the sexual instincts are taken up into it—component parts of the erotic interest—that are more or less clearly visible in childhood and are invariably discovered in the neurotic by psychoanalysis in later years. This tender feeling represents the earliest childish choice of object. From this we see that the sexual instincts find their first *objects* along the path laid down by the ego instincts and in accordance with the value set by the latter on their objects, in just the same way that the first sexual *satisfactions* are experienced, i.e., in connection with the bodily functions necessary for self-preservation. The "affection" shown to the child by its parents and attendants, which seldom fails to betray its erotic character ("a child is an erotic plaything"), does a great deal to increase the erotic contributions to the cathexes that are put forth by the ego instincts in the child, and to raise them to a level that is bound to leave its mark on future development, especially when certain other circumstances leading to the same result are present.

These fixations of the child's feelings of affection are maintained through childhood, continually absorbing erotic elements, which are thus deflected from their sexual aims. Then, when the age of puberty is reached, there supervenes upon this state of things a powerful current of "sensual" feeling the aims of which can no longer be disguised. It never fails, apparently, to pursue the earlier paths and to invest the objects of the primary infantile choice with currents of libido that are now far stronger. But in relation to these objects it is confronted by the obstacle of the incest barrier that has in the meanwhile been erected; consequently it seeks as soon as possible to pass on from these objects unsuited for real satisfaction to others in the world outside, with whom a real sexual life may be carried on. These new objects are still chosen after the pattern (imago) of the infantile ones; in time, however, they attract to themselves the tender feeling that had been anchored to those others. A man shall leave father and mother—according to the biblical precept—and cleave to his wife; then are tenderness and sensuality united. The greatest intensity of sensual passion will bring with it the highest mental estimation of the object (the normal overestimation of the sexual object characteristic of men).

Two factors will determine whether this advance in the development of the libido is accomplished successfully or otherwise. First, there is the degree of frustration in reality that is opposed to the new object-choice and reduces its value for the person concerned. For there is no sense in entering upon a choice of object if one is not to be allowed to choose at all or has no prospect of being able to choose one fit for the part. The second factor is the degree of attraction that may be exercised by the infantile objects that should be relinquished, and this is proportionate to the erotic cathexis already attaching to them in childhood. If these two factors are sufficiently powerful, the general mechanism leading to the formation of neurosis will come into operation. The libido turns away from reality and is absorbed into the creation of fantasy (introversion), strengthens the images of the first sexual objects, and becomes fixated to them. The incest barrier, however, necessarily has the effect that the libido attaching to these objects should remain in the unconscious. The sensual current of feeling is now attached to unconscious ideas of objects, and discharge of it in onanistic acts contributes to a strengthening of this fixation. It constitutes no change in this state of affairs if the step forward to extraneous objects that miscarried in reality is now made in fantasy, if in the fantasied situations leading up to onanistic gratification the extraneous objects are but replacements of the original ones. The fantasies become capable of entering consciousness by this replacement, but in the direction of applying the libido externally in the real world no advance has been made.

In this way it may happen that the whole current of sensual feeling in a young man may remain attached in the unconscious to incestuous objects, or, to put it in another way, may be fixated to incestuous fantasies. The result of this is then total impotence, which is perhaps even reinforced by an actual weakening, developing concurrently, of the organs destined to execute the sexual act.

Less severe conditions will suffice to bring about what is usually called psychical impotence. It is not necessary that the whole amount of sensual feeling should be fated to conceal itself behind the tender feelings; it may remain sufficiently strong and unchecked to secure some outlet for itself in reality. The sexual activity of such people shows unmistakable signs, however, that it has not behind it the whole mental energy belonging to the instinct. It is capricious, easily upset, often clumsily carried out, and not very pleasurable. Above all, however, it avoids all association with feelings of tenderness. A restriction has thus been laid upon the object-choice. The sensual feeling that has remained active seeks only objects evoking no reminder of the incestuous persons forbidden to it; the impression made by someone who seems deserving of high estimation leads, not to a sensual excitation, but to feelings of tenderness that remain erotically ineffectual. The erotic life of such people remains dissociated, divided between two channels, the same two that are personified in art as heavenly and earthly (or animal) love. Where such men love they have no desire and where they desire they cannot love. In order to keep their sensuality out of contact with the objects they love, they seek out objects whom they need not love; and, in accordance with the laws of the "sensitivity of complexes" and the "return of the repressed," the strange refusal implied in psychical impotence is made whenever the objects selected in order to avoid incest possess some trait, often quite inconspicuous, reminiscent of the objects that must be avoided.

The principal means of protection used by men against this complaint consists in *lowering* the sexual object in their own estimation, while reserving for the incestuous object and for those who represent it the over-estimation normally felt for the sexual object. As soon as the sexual object fulfills the condition of being degraded, sensual feeling can have free play; considerable sexual capacity and a high degree of pleasure can be developed. Another factor also contributes to this result. There is usually little refinement in the ways of obtaining erotic pleasure habitual to people in whom the tender and the sensual currents of feeling are not properly merged; they have remained addicted to perverse sexual aims that they feel it a considerable deprivation not to gratify, yet to such men this seems possible only with a sexual object who in their estimate is degraded and worth little.

The motives behind the fantasies mentioned in the preceding paper, by which boys degrade the mother to the level of a prostitute, now become intelligible. They represent efforts to bridge the gulf between the two currents of erotic feeling, at least in fantasy: by degrading her, to win the mother as an object for sensual desires.

2

So far we have pursued our inquiry into psychical impotence from a medico-psychological angle that is not justified by the title of this paper. It will prove, however, that this introduction was necessary in order to provide an approach to our actual theme.

We have reduced psychical impotence to a disunion between the tender and sensual currents of erotic feeling, and have explained this inhibition in development itself as an effect of strong fixations in childhood and of frustration in reality later, after the incest barrier has intervened. There is one principal objection to raise against this doctrine: it does too much, it explains why certain persons suffer from psychical impotence, but it makes it seem puzzling that others can escape the affliction. Since all the factors that appear to be involved—the strong fixation in childhood, the incest barrier, and the frustration in the years of development after puberty—are demonstrably present in practically all civilized persons, one would be justified in expecting that psychical impotence was universally prevalent in civilized countries and not a disease of particular individuals.

It would not be difficult to escape from this conclusion by pointing to the quantitative element in the causation of disease, that greater or lesser amount of each single factor that determines whether or not recognizable disease results. But although this argument is in my opinion sound, I do not myself intend to employ it in refuting the objection advanced above. I shall, on the contrary, put forward the proposition that psychical impotence is far more widespread than is generally supposed, and that some degree of this condition does in fact characterize the erotic life of civilized peoples.

If one enlarges the meaning of the term psychical impotence, and ceases to limit it to failure to perform the act of coitus, although an intention to derive pleasure from it is present and the genital apparatus is intact, it would comprise, to begin with, all those men who are described as psycho-anaesthetic, i.e., who never fail in the act but who perform it without special pleasure—a state of things that is commoner than one might think.

Psychoanalytic study of such cases has discovered the same etiological factors in them as those found in psychical impotence, when employed in the narrower sense, without at first discovering any explanation of the symptomatic difference between the two. By an analogy that is easy to justify, one is led on from these anaesthetic men to consider the enormous number of frigid women, whose attitude to love can in fact not be described or understood better than by equating it with psychical impotence in men, although the latter is more conspicuous.

If, however, instead of attributing a wide significance to the term psychical impotence, we look about for instances of its peculiar symptomatology in less marked forms, we shall not be able to deny that the behavior in love of the men of present-day civilization bears in general the character of the psychically impotent type. In only very few people of culture are the two strains of tenderness and sensuality duly fused into one; the man almost always feels his sexual activity hampered by his respect for the woman and only develops full sexual potency when he finds himself in the presence of a lower type of sexual object; and this again is partly conditioned by the circumstance that his sexual aims include those of perverse sexual components, which he does not like to gratify with a woman he respects. Full sexual satisfaction only comes when he can give himself up wholeheartedly to enjoyment, which with his well-brought-up wife, for instance, he does not venture to do. Hence comes his need for a less exalted sexual object, a woman ethically inferior, to whom he need ascribe no aesthetic misgivings, and who does not know the rest of his life and cannot criticize him. It is to such a woman that he prefers to devote his sexual potency, even when all the tenderness in him belongs to one of a higher type. It is possible, too, that the tendency so often observed in men of the highest rank in society to take a woman of a low class as a permanent mistress, or even as a wife, is nothing but a consequence of the need for a lower type of sexual object on which, psychologically, the possibility of complete gratification depends.

I do not hesitate to lay the responsibility also for this very common condition in the erotic life of civilized men on the two factors operative in absolute psychical impotence, namely, the very strong incestuous fixation of childhood and the frustration by reality suffered during adolescence. It has an ugly sound and a paradoxical sound as well, but nevertheless it must be said that whoever is to be really free and happy in love must have overcome his deference for women and come to terms with the idea of incest with mother or sister. Anyone who in the face of this test subjects himself to serious self-examination will indubitably find that at the bottom of his heart he too regards the sexual act as something degrading, which soils and contaminates not only the body. And he will only be able to look for the origin of this attitude, which he will certainly not willingly acknowledge, in that period of his youth in which his sexual passions are already strongly developed but in which gratification of them with an object outside the family was almost as completely prohibited as with an incestuous one.

The women of our civilized world are similarly affected by their upbringing and further, too, by the reaction upon them of this attitude in men. Naturally the effect upon a woman is just as unfavorable if the man comes to her without his full potency as if, after overestimating her in the early stages of falling in love, he then, having successfully possessed himself of her, sets her at naught. Women show little need to degrade the sexual object; no doubt this has some connection with the circumstance that as a rule they develop little of the sexual overestimation natural to men. The long abstinence from sexuality to which they are forced and the lingering of their sensuality in fantasy have in them, however, another important consequence. It is often not possible for them later on to undo the connection thus formed in their minds between sensual activities and something forbidden, and they turn out to be psychically impotent, i.e., frigid, when at last such activities do become permissible. This is the source of the desire in so many women to keep even legitimate relations secret for a time; and of the appearance of the capacity for normal sensation in others as soon as the condition of prohibition is restored by a secret intrigue—untrue to the husband, they can keep a second order of faith with the lover.

In my opinion the necessary condition of forbiddenness in the erotic life of women holds the same place as the man's need to lower his sexual object. Both are the consequence of the long period of delay between sexual maturity and sexual activity that is demanded by education for social reasons. The aim of both is to overcome the psychical impotence resulting from the lack of union between tenderness and sensuality. That the effect of the same causes differs so greatly in men and in women is perhaps due to another difference in the behavior of the two sexes. Women belonging to the higher levels of civilization do not usually transgress the prohibition against sexual activities during the period of waiting, and thus they acquire this close association between the forbidden and the sexual. Men usually overstep the prohibition under the condition of lowering the standard of object they require, and so carry this condition on into their subsequent erotic life.

In view of the strenuous efforts being made in the civilized world at the present day to reform sexual life, it is not superfluous to remind the reader that psychoanalytic investigations have no more bias in any direction than has any other scientific research. In tracing back to its concealed sources what is manifest, psychoanalysis has no aim but that of disclosing connections. It can but be satisfied if what it has brought to light is of use in effecting reforms by substituting more advantageous for injurious conditions. It cannot, however, predict whether other, perhaps even greater, sacrifices may not result from other institutions.

3

The fact that the restrictions imposed by cultural education upon erotic life involve a general lowering of the sexual object may prompt us to turn our eyes from the object to the instincts themselves. The injurious results of the deprivation of sexual enjoyment at the beginning manifest themselves in lack of full satisfaction when sexual desire is later given free rein in marriage. But, on the other hand, unrestrained sexual liberty from the beginning leads to no better result. It is easy to show that the value the mind sets on erotic needs instantly sinks as soon as satisfaction becomes readily obtainable. Some obstacle is necessary to swell the tide of the libido to its height; and at all periods of history, wherever natural barriers in the way of satisfaction have not sufficed, mankind has erected conventional ones in order to be able to enjoy love. This is true both of individuals and of nations. In times during which no obstacles to sexual satisfaction existed, such as, may be, during the decline of the civilizations of antiquity, love became worthless, life became empty, and strong reaction-formations were necessary before the indispensable emotional value of love could be recovered. In this context it may be stated that the ascetic tendency of Christianity had the effect of raising the psychical value of love in a way that heathen antiquity could never achieve; it developed greatest significance in the lives of the ascetic monks, which were almost entirely occupied with struggles against libidinous temptation.

One's first inclination undoubtedly is to see in this difficulty a universal characteristic of our organic instincts. It is certainly true in a general way that the importance of an instinctual desire is mentally increased by frustration of it. Suppose one made the experiment of exposing a number of utterly different human beings to hunger under the same conditions. As the imperative need for food rose in them all their individual differences would be effaced, and instead the uniform manifestations of one unsatisfied instinct would appear. But is it also true, conversely, that the mental value of an instinct invariably sinks with gratification of it? One thinks, for instance, of the relation of the wine drinker to wine. Is it not a fact that wine always affords the drinker the same toxic satisfaction—one that in poetry has so often been likened to the erotic and that science as well may regard as comparable? Has one ever heard of a drinker being forced constantly to change his wine because he soon gets tired of always drinking the same? On the contrary, habit binds a man more and more to the particular kind of wine he drinks. Do we ever find a drinker impelled to go to another country where the wine is dearer or where alcohol is prohibited, in order to stimulate his dwindling pleasure in it by these obstacles? Nothing of the sort. If we listen to what our great lovers of alcohol say about their attitude to wine, for instance, B. Böcklin, it sounds like the most perfect harmony, a model of a happy marriage. Why is the relation of the lover to his sexual object so very different?

However strange it may sound, I think the possibility must be considered that something in the nature of the sexual instinct itself is unfavorable to the achievement of absolute gratification. When we think of the long and difficult evolution the instinct goes through, two factors to which this difficulty might be ascribed at once emerge. First, in consequence of the two "thrusts" of sexual development impelling towards choice of an object, together with the intervention of the incest barrier between the two, the ultimate object selected is never the original one but only a surrogate for it. Psychoanalysis has shown us, however, that when the original object of an instinctual desire becomes lost in consequence of repression, it is often replaced by an endless series of substitute objects, none of which ever give full satisfaction. This may explain the lack of stability in object-choice, the "craving for stimulus," which is so often a feature of the love of adults.

Secondly, we know that at its beginning the sexual instinct is divided into a large number of components—or, rather, it develops from them—not all of which can be carried on into its final form; some have to be suppressed or turned to other uses before the final form results. Above all, the coprophilic elements in the instinct have proved incompatible with our aesthetic ideas, probably since the time when man developed an upright posture and so removed his organ of smell from the ground; further, a considerable proportion of the sadistic elements belonging to the erotic instinct have to be abandoned. All such developmental processes, however, relate only to the upper layers of the complicated structure. The fundamental processes that promote erotic excitation remain always the same. Excremental things are all too intimately and inseparably bound up with sexual things; the position of the genital organs—*inter urinas et faeces*—remains the decisive and unchangeable factor. One might say, modifying a well-known saying of the great Napolean's, "Anatomy is destiny." The genitals themselves have not undergone the development of the rest of the human form in the direction of beauty; they have retained their animal cast; and so even today love, too, is in essence as animal as it ever was. The erotic instincts are hard to mold; training to them achieves now too much, now too little. What culture tries to make out of them seems attainable only at the cost of a sensible loss of pleasure; the persistence of the impulses that are not enrolled in adult sexual activity makes itself felt in an absence of satisfaction.

So perhaps we must make up our minds to the idea that altogether it is not possible for the claims of the sexual instinct to be reconciled with the demands of culture, that in consequence of his cultural development, renunciation, and suffering, as well as the danger of his extinction at some far future time, are not to be eluded by the race of man. This gloomy prognosis rests, it is true, on the single conjecture that the lack of satisfaction accompanying culture is the necessary consequence of certain peculiarities developed by the sexual instinct under the pressure of culture. This very incapacity in the sexual instinct to yield full satisfaction as soon as it submits to the first demands of culture becomes the source, however, of the grandest cultural achievements, which are brought to birth by ever greater sublimation of the components of the sexual instinct. For what motive would induce man to put his sexual energy to other uses if by any disposal of it he could obtain fully satisfying pleasure? He would never let go of this pleasure and would make no further progress. It seems, therefore, that the irreconcilable antagonism between the demands of the two instincts—the sexual and the egoistic—have made man capable of ever greater achievements, though, it is true, under the continual menace of danger, such as that of the neuroses to which at the present time the weaker are succumbing.

The purpose of science is neither to alarm nor to reassure. But I myself freely admit that such far-reaching conclusions as those drawn here should be built up on a broader foundation, and that perhaps developments in other directions will enable mankind to remedy the effects of these, which we have here been considering in isolation.

FOR DISCUSSION

1. According to Freud, why are some men capable of sexual pleasure only when the object of their sexual desire is degraded? What does Freud mean by "degraded"? (24)
2. What does Freud mean when he says that "this introduction was necessary in order to provide an approach to our actual theme"? What is his "actual theme"? (24)
3. Why does Freud make a distinction between the psychical impotence of men and of women?
4. At the end of the essay, what is Freud's attitude toward the "grandest cultural achievements" of humankind that he says result from the "sublimation of the components of the sexual instinct"? (32)

FOR FURTHER REFLECTION

1. Does Freud think that the union between tenderness and sensuality, which he says constitutes "a fully normal attitude in love," is ever possible for civilized persons? Since he believes that "psychical impotence," for both men and women, is so prevalent in civilized culture, how can he define what is "normal"? (20)
2. Are Freud's observations about the inhibitions imposed on sexual expression by the civilized world universally true? How are they accurate or not for you today?

Fay Weldon (1931–) was born in England and grew up in New Zealand. Her father, a doctor, and her mother, a writer, divorced when she was five. Weldon attended the University of St. Andrew's in Scotland, where she studied economics and psychology. She spent her twenties and thirties in various jobs before developing a successful career as an advertising copywriter. In the early 1960s, Weldon left advertising to pursue her own writing. She has since published numerous novels, plays, television and radio scripts, and short stories. Recent novels include *She May Not Leave* (2005), *The Spa* (2007), *The Stepmother's Diary* (2008), and *The Chalcot Crescent* (2009). "Sex" is taken from *What Makes Women Happy* (2006), described in a *Booklist* review as "part memoir, part self-help guide." Weldon lives in Dorset, England, and teaches creative writing at Brunel University.

Sex
(selection)

Sources of Envy

> 10 percent of women never experience orgasm.
> 20 percent occasionally do.
> 50 percent sometimes do.
> 20 percent usually do.
> 10 percent always do.

Or so the current figures say. But figures change. Someone in the 10 percent "always" category suddenly goes down to the next division: "*My partner came back from his trip and he'd grown a beard.*" Someone in the "never" group claims now to be in the "sometimes" category: "*I met another man.*" But the broad pattern is clear. The pleasure so liberally bestowed upon men by nature is only grudgingly given to women.

Of course women resent it. Listen to any conversation between women when men aren't there: at the hen night, on the factory floor, over the garden fence, at the English Lit. tutorial. Women may laugh and joke, but actually they're furious. "*They can, we can't, unfair, unfair.*" They may not know what's biting them, but that's it.

But facts are facts and there we are. Deal with it. Life is not fair. Resenting the fact is no recipe for happiness.

. . .

Indeed, the less you think about orgasms the better, since the greatest bar to having one, if we're to believe the research, is wanting one. Best if they creep up on you unawares. Women are at their most orgasmic when they are least anxious, but wondering why you're not having one can make you very anxious indeed. Which is ironic, since what you want most you're going to get least.

But a lot of life is like that. Want too much and it's snatched away. An attitude of careless insouciance is more likely to pay dividends.

Because really, having an orgasm or not doesn't matter in the great scheme of things, just as having an éclair or not doesn't matter. Life goes on pretty much the same with or without. There are other pleasures. There's true love, trust, and sensual pleasure. Or, if you're that kind of person, and I hope you are not, the victory of disdain. "*See, knew you were no good in bed.*"

But actually, it's as likely, if not more likely, to be your doing, not his.

Unfair—but what you are after is happiness. Sexual repletion is not a necessary ingredient. Sexual satisfaction can happen anyway, and is not dependent on orgasm. If women were not so often described as "achieving orgasm" then there would be no sense of failure when they didn't. The word is wrong, not the thing itself.

"*I don't do orgasm*" might be a more useful way of describing yourself, initially, to a partner, and it's a bonus to both if it turns out not to be true. But having an orgasm is not a sign of true love any more than the lack of it is the opposite. I have read letters from girls who think they must end a relationship because sex between them and their true love does not conclude with an orgasm for her. Imagining sex has failed, they feel the relationship has failed. It hasn't—all that has happened has been that she *didn't have an orgasm*. So what? Better, more conducive to happiness, just to see orgasm as an additional extra, something special that happens, a bonus, a surprising gift from heaven which descends like manna from time to time, not your natural-born right—and then a whole raft of unhappiness will be wiped from your life.

In Any Case

Female orgasm has no apparent usefulness to the human race. This puzzles those who think that everything in nature has to have a purpose, those who personalize evolution as if it knew what it was doing and had some end of perfection in sight. Some say muscular spasms help the sperm on its way to the egg; others doubt it. It is not the longing for orgasm which makes the virgin girl fall in love—though it may be the boy's. Another inequality, another injustice!

The peacock's tail demonstrates sexual attraction in overdose as he struts before the female; his voice would be enough to put anyone off. I don't suppose nature was after fairness, trying to balance things in the scales of justice, when she gave with one hand and took away with the other.

Why different birds have different voices no one knows—and no one's worked out what they're *for*—but those with (to our ears) the sweetest voices are the ones who sing the loudest and seem to relish their singing most. I like to think that the thrushes in my garden sing because it occurs to them that it's a beautiful morning and they feel like acknowledging it. It's an irrational thought, but it makes me happy for at least ten minutes, wandering in the garden and listening, but then the sun gets too hot and I worry because I haven't got a hat.

Some say that, like male nipples and the appendix, female orgasm is a mistake which nature has failed to recognize as a nonnecessity. Better to see it as a celebration and a reward just for being alive. But there are others—the exhilaration of ideas, conversations, the company of good friends and so on—which probably add up to more.

The Joy of the Fake Orgasm

Just fake. Happy, generous-minded women, not too hung up about emotional honesty, fake. Research tells us that when you do there is "*activity in the part of the motor cortex that relates to the genitals, the amygdala, but not the deactivation of the cerebral cortex that occurs prior and after a genuine orgasm.*" In other words you have to be happy to have an orgasm, but if you have an orgasm you will be happy.

Activate the positive. Deactivate the negative. That's what it's all about.

The more highly educated you are, the more likely you are to fake orgasm. I am not sure what we deduce from that. Is too much intellectual stimulation bad for the love life? Or does it just occur to clever women pretty soon that it's only sensible to fake it?

Genuine orgasm experienced, acknowledged, and stored away as one of the uncompromisingly good things in life, you will then no doubt leap out of bed and make breakfast, or squeeze orange juice or pour champagne or whatever your lifestyle, with the words "*You are so clever,*" or however you express enthusiasm, ringing in his—or her, of course, should you be a lesbian—ears.

If you are sensible you will do exactly the same if you've faked it, because half the pleasure of sex is being nice to the other person, and half is better than none, on the half-full, half-empty cup principle. Clever, judgemental, honourable people who feel deception is unworthy of them, who say, "*But relationships must be based upon truth,*" are likely to be of the half-empty sort.

Remember you are not in pursuit of justice, you are seeking what makes women happy. You must catch it as it flies, and if it flies just out of reach, well, it was a nice sight while it lasted, wasn't it?

Faking is kind to male partners of the new man kind, who like to think they have done their duty by you. Otherwise they too may become anxious and so less able to perform. The more the woman rates "performance," the more likely the man is to wilt and fail. Do yourself and him a favour, sister: fake it. Then, who knows, as a reward for your kindness, sublime pleasure may creep up on you unawares.

There is a great confusion here between the pleasures of love and the pleasures of sex. Both can carry on along parallel tracks, never touching, to the end of time. Or one day, who's to say, they may meet.

My friend Olivia, now 69, had an orgasm for the first time when she was 54 and nine years into her second marriage. It took her by surprise. But she said it was like learning to ride a bicycle: once you knew how to do it, you could do it all the time. She's been clocking them up ever since. Life does not begin at 20. She was doing well enough without them, was earning a salary at that time as CEO of a media communications firm and had seemed to me to be living a full, even overfull, love life since I first met her when she was 18.

Her first marriage ended in scandal and divorce—her husband, a writer, naming seven co-respondents. (In those days of guilty and innocent, sexual infidelity had to be proved. Illicit couples had to be discovered *in flagrante*, stained sheets produced and so on, before the judge would grant a divorce.) The press went to town. Oddly enough, the naming and shaming did Olivia no harm in the business world. Even then, everyone liked anyone who had their name in the papers. And then the sixties were upon us and a great deal of random sexual activity went on as a matter of course, and after that divorce was not a matter of right or wrong but about the division of property. Meanwhile Olivia rose rocket-like through the corporate world and who is to say, if she had had more orgasms, she would have bothered to reach such heights? A touch of discontent in the night may be good for all of us. Sexual satisfaction, sensual repletion, and the irrational sense of gratitude which tends to go with them, may be the last thing a career woman needs.

Most women, I suspect, are after true love, rather than orgasm, though they will put up with many stages on the way, from pure lust to pride assuaged to boredom endured. And even if true love is not on your agenda, it is always gratifying to stir it in others. If faking it helps, do it.

The Naturalness of the Hen Night

Girls together is good, girls together is fun and usually noisy. But notice how bitterness against men seems to be hardwired, as if nature had bred us to be suspicious of the male, on the lookout for bad behavior. There's something in us of the female cat, not letting the tom near the kittens in case he eats them. Put us together and there's no stopping us. Listen in to the talk and laughter at a girls' night out: anecdotes about the follies of men, jokes about the minimal size of their parts, tales of male vanity and self-delusion—their stumbling mumbleness, their crazy driving.

We egg each other on to disloyalty. We are the women; we close ranks in opposition to men. The food gets cold on the plate in our excitement. The wine is quickly drunk, and more wine, and vodka shorts. We are the Maenads just before Orpheus comes on the scene to get torn to bits.

And then the mirth gets bitter. It isn't really funny, it's real. Someone begins to cry.

Men who leave, men who won't leave, men who fail to provide, men who don't love you after all, men who are a sexual disappointment. Past husbands, vanished partners, the ones who never washed, the ones who had the *au-pair* girl. Men: ridiculous, pathetic, sad.

The noise diminishes and fades away. Silence falls. Time to count heads and divide the bill. Those who have partners slip away, feeling guilty and grateful. Those who haven't go home on their own, or walk each other to the bus, and tell themselves all they need is their friends.

. . .

I have in my time enjoyed such gatherings immensely. They are a great pleasure. Life is good. The trick is to pay and leave just before the silence falls. And try not to be the one collecting the money and tipping the waiter.

Go to Norway and Sweden and notice how the restaurants are full of men. Few women eat out. Yet in theory these are super-equal societies. The women, one supposes, can only prefer to stay at home. These all-male meals—tables for four, six, eight, ten, more—tend to be silent, grim affairs. Men like to sit side by side, silently, metaphorically locking horns, and don't seem to have nearly such a good time as women do. But they do seem to get happier as the evening progresses, not the other way around. Life gets better, not worse. It isn't fair.

Nothing's fair.

It's unfair that some people like sex a lot, some very little, some not at all. The capacity for pleasure is not doled out equally or fairly.

> (Is it probably a good idea that people with equivalent levels of sexual energy partner one another, if they want the union to last. People need to wear each other out in bed. Three times a day, three times a week (the norm), or once a year—so long as both are suited, what's the worry?)

Mind you, the easy-orgasmers, the lucky 20 percent, are not always popular with others. The papers this morning were in a state of outrage about Sandy, a feckless girl of 19 who went on holiday to Spain leaving her three children in the care of a 15-year-old. When summonsed home by the police and the media, she refused to go. She was having too good a time, she said. She had her photo taken burying her head into the bare chest of a semi-naked waiter. I bet she had orgasms at the drop of a hat. She knew how to enjoy herself. She was not anxious. She did not feel guilt. She well and truly broke the ten-minute rule. She stretched it to a whole week of drink, drugs, sex, and ecstasy before guilt set in and she flew home. That's one way of doing it.

It Isn't Fair But It's a Fact

The fight for gender equality is bad for the looks. It makes no one happy, unless you find some reward in struggling for a justice that evolution failed to deliver. It will just develop your jaw, wrinkle your brow beyond the capacity of Botox to unravel, muddy your complexion so much that no amount of Beauty Flash will clear it, and in general do you no good.

Fight for political justice by all means—join the party, reform and re-educate. Fight for domestic justice—"*Your turn to clean the loo*"—if you must, though personally I don't recommend too much of it, it's too exhausting. But do not fight for physiological equality because it does not exist.

If you have a period pain, you have one. Accept it. Don't fight it. Sit down. Take a pill. A male voice raised is impressive; a female voice raised creates antipathy. Accept it. You are not trying to be a man. You are proud to be a woman. Do not shout your enemies down at the client meeting—leave that to the men. Get your way by smiling sweetly. The end is more important than the means.

Accept that for women happiness comes in short bursts and the ten-minute rule applies. For men it can last as long as a football match before they realize they're late picking up the child from school.

So is the sum of human happiness greater for a man than for a woman? I suspect so. Lucky old them.

Be generous. You can afford to be. At least you occupy the moral high ground, and they know it.

Occupying the Moral High Ground

It's quite nice up here these days. Women can look out over the urban landscape and know they are nicer than men, more cooperative, more empathic, better at communication, better at getting to university, and better at getting jobs. Women multitask—everyone knows. They can do many things at once. Men tend to do one thing at a time. If a woman loses a sock she finds another which will do just as well; a man continues the search until he has found it (albeit in the bin where he threw it), by which time the train has gone and the meeting has begun.

Women abjure the idle languorousness of sexual contentment and get on with things. Women leap out of bed after sex to feed the cat and wash out their smalls so that they'll be dry by morning. Men just go to sleep gratified and satisfied, happy that all is well. (Though if it's not his own bed he may well want to regain it before falling asleep. "*I'll call you in the morning*," he says. Oh yes!)

. . .

Women worry in advance. They search through their bags for the dry-cleaning ticket before they even get into the shop. Men wait until they're in there and then hold everyone up.

Just Accept It

Accept gender differences, don't deny them. That way you make the most of what happiness nature did allow you as a woman.

Evolution has allowed you an intellect that's pretty much the same as the male's.

> (Though the male bell curve when it comes to IQ is a little more flattened than for the female. That is to say there are more males at the extreme ends of the spectrum—extreme intelligence, extreme lack of it—which is why you get more male double-firsts at Oxford than female and more males held in police cells overnight than females.)

Evolution has also allowed you an aesthetic appreciation equal to that of a male. There are as many men as women listening to flute concertos at the Wigmore Hall, as many men as women wandering round art galleries.

> (Nature might slightly favour the male when it comes to creative activity—men's books may be "better," if less readable, than women's, their paintings fetch more in the art market, and so on—but that claim would take a whole book on its own to discuss.)

. . .

The traditionally female qualities of caring and nurturing, sharing and cooperating, were not always seen as admirable. Inside the home a woman did them for free; outside the home they commanded low wages. Society favoured to male virtues: dismissing and disposing, self-control and a stiff upper lip. But then women, released by technological advance from the domestic drudgery required just to keep the children alive, have used their new power brilliantly. Theirs are the qualities now most valued in Western society. Forget the old male values of never apologizing, never explaining—they're outmoded. Presidents weep, prime ministers apologize, monarchs explain.

To have to accept your genetic make-up, the femaleness of your body, its irritating habit of keeping menstrual time with the moon, is not so bad a fate. These cosmic forces are too great for you to take on single-handed anyway.

It isn't fair, but it's a fact.

If It Takes a Man to Make You Happy . . .

It's a dreadful assumption to make that just because a woman is a woman she must need a man. I know many a female who's lived happily ever after without one. They may well have a blip in their midforties when it occurs to them that being single looks like being a permanent state. That pang of doubt is nature's last-ditch stand against the nurture that persuades a woman that a man is an optional extra. But the automatic, instinctive pairings-off of the under-thirties are a long way behind her now. Crowded rooms are not for looking across in case she sees the man of her dreams, but for meeting friends, elegant conversation, and making useful business contacts. She is the contented singleton. She tried sex and found it wanting. She never met a man she liked or respected enough to join forces with on a permanent basis. She has money enough to enjoy her life.

My mother, coming from a generation in which any man was better than none, would have described her as "too picky." And today's educated young woman is certainly in something of a pickle, what with both nature (her traditional selectivity when it comes to choosing a mate) and nurture (our current understanding that compared to women men are crude, loud-voiced, doltish creatures; look at any TV ad to see it) persuading her that nothing but a truly alpha male will do for her. That knight in shining armour crashing through the undergrowth to find her has to be better born than she is, better educated, and richer—women have such a passion for marrying their superiors—and it gets harder and harder to find such a man.

And the girls of the tribe, the ones in her age group, will be watching and vetting to make sure she gets it right.

"*You can do better than that,*" they'll say. (That's tribe-talk too. Friends as arbiters of sexual choice is a timeless scenario.) Their judgement these days isn't so good, that's the trouble. It's self-conscious, and probably self-interested too. They need someone to sit next to in the cinema, to laugh and giggle with. The pleasures of a night out with friends outweigh the pleasures of a date. Men just look at films and grunt; girls *talk*.

. . .

But anyway, here she is, and life is good, and what should she want with a man? If she needs to change a tyre she can use her mobile and call a garage. Once she had to stand by the side of the road showing a leg. (She could do it herself, but whoever wanted to do that? My dear, the oil, the spanners, the weakness of the unaccustomed wrist!) The pang soon fades. She is happy again, and good for her.

But if you still believe that only with a man can you be truly happy, then you had better find one.

Finding a Man

There are two ways of doing it:

1. *He chases and you run.* This requires nerve, and you to be higher on the scale of partner-desirability than he. If you are convinced that you are—your beauty outweighing his wealth, for example—then give it a go. Female disdain is attractive, but you have to have looks to get away with it. Your handbook will be *The Rules.*

2. *You sit quiet and smile.* Never when in the company of the man you're after do you give him a hard time. You never argue, quarrel, demand your rights, reproach him, give him one iota of emotional, intellectual, or physical discomfort. This is the best ploy for the 80 percent of women who were not born with symmetrical features and a sexy body, who have wiry hair and a muddy complexion and cannot be bothered to have cosmetic surgery. Your handbook will be *The Surrendered Wife.*

. . .

A man, research tells us, plays the sexual field until he decides he's ready to settle down. Then he looks round the field of his female acquaintance and picks the one he likes the most. Let it be you. If that's what you want.

A woman, research tells us, goes searching for the perfect mate within her field of expectation (the rich marry the rich, remember, the beautiful the beautiful) and may go on searching too long. Her vision of herself can be inflated ("*Because I'm worth it!*"), her standards higher than is practical. That is why we have so many talented, beautiful, high-earning, intelligent, single young women about, while their male compatriots are safely tucked away in the suburbs, shacked up with some dim and dozy wife. Too picky!

Category 2 women fail when they behave as if they were in category 1. Only in romantic novels does Mr. Darcy marry Elizabeth Bennett. He ran, she ran faster, he turned round and caught her. In real life he might have set her up as his mistress in Maida Vale, but marriage? No. On the scale of partner-desirability they did not match.

FOR DISCUSSION

1. When Weldon speaks of orgasm, why does she say, "The word is wrong, not the thing itself"? (38)
2. What justification does Weldon offer for introducing deception into intimate relationships by faking orgasm?
3. Why does Weldon think that "sexual satisfaction . . . may be the last thing a career woman needs"? (42)
4. What is Weldon recommending to women when she says, "Accept gender differences, don't deny them"? (47)

FOR FURTHER REFLECTION

1. According to Weldon, what is it that "makes women happy"? (41) Do you agree with her?
2. What is Weldon's point in giving advice on finding a man? In light of the rest of her essay, how seriously does she intend this advice to be taken?

Margaret Atwood (1939–) was born in Ottawa and grew up in northern Ontario, Quebec, and Toronto. She attended Victoria College at the University of Toronto and received a master's degree in English literature from Radcliffe College. Atwood is the author of more than thirty-five volumes of poetry, children's literature, fiction, and nonfiction. Her novels include *The Handmaid's Tale* (1985), winner of the Governor General's Literary Award for Fiction, Canada's foremost literary prize; *The Blind Assassin* (2000), which won the Booker Prize; and *The Year of the Flood* (2009). The poem "Helen of Troy Does Counter Dancing" was first published in 1995 in her poetry anthology *Morning in the Burned House*. Atwood has taught English and served as writer-in-residence at universities in Canada, the United States, and Australia. She currently resides in Toronto.

Helen of Troy Does Counter Dancing

The world is full of women
who'd tell me I should be ashamed of myself
if they had the chance. Quit dancing.
Get some self-respect
and a day job.
Right. And minimum wage,
and varicose veins, just standing
in one place for eight hours
behind a glass counter
bundled up to the neck, instead of
naked as a meat sandwich.
Selling gloves, or something.
Instead of what I do sell.
You have to have talent
to peddle a thing so nebulous
and without material form.
Exploited, they'd say. Yes, any way
you cut it, but I've a choice
of how, and I'll take the money.
I do give value.
Like preachers, I sell vision,
like perfume ads, desire
or its facsimile. Like jokes
or war, it's all in the timing.
I sell men back their worst suspicions:
that everything's for sale,
and piecemeal. They gaze at me and see
a chain-saw murder just before it happens,

when thigh, ass, inkblot, crevice, tit, and nipple
are still connected.
Such hatred leaps in them,
my beery worshippers! That, or a bleary
hopeless love. Seeing the rows of heads
and upturned eyes, imploring
but ready to snap at my ankles,
I understand floods and earthquakes, and the urge
to step on ants. I keep the beat,
and dance for them because
they can't. The music smells like foxes,
crisp as heated metal
searing the nostrils
or humid as August, hazy and languorous
as a looted city the day after,
when all the rape's been done
already, and the killing,
and the survivors wander around
looking for garbage
to eat, and there's only a bleak exhaustion.

Speaking of which, it's the smiling
tires me out the most.
This, and the pretence
that I can't hear them.
And I can't, because I'm after all
a foreigner to them.
The speech here is all warty gutturals,
obvious as a slab of ham,
but I come from the province of the gods
where meanings are lilting and oblique.
I don't let on to everyone,
but lean close, and I'll whisper:
My mother was raped by a holy swan.
You believe that? You can take me out to dinner.

That's what we tell all the husbands.
There sure are a lot of dangerous birds around.

Not that anyone here
but you would understand.
The rest of them would like to watch me
and feel nothing. Reduce me to components
as in a clock factory or abattoir.
Crush out the mystery.
Wall me up alive
in my own body.
They'd like to see through me,
but nothing is more opaque
than absolute transparency.
Look—my feet don't hit the marble!
Like breath or a balloon, I'm rising,
I hover six inches in the air
in my blazing swan-egg of light.
You think I'm not a goddess?
Try me.
This is a torch song.
Touch me and you'll burn.

FOR DISCUSSION

1. Why does the poem begin with the speaker saying that the world is full of women "who'd tell me I should be ashamed of myself / if they had the chance"? (55) Why does the speaker reject the kinds of work she imagines these women urging on her?
2. Why does the speaker "sell men back their worst suspicions"? (55) Why does she continue dancing for men she believes harbor violent fantasies and hatred toward her?
3. What does the speaker mean when she says that the men can't see through her because "nothing is more opaque / than absolute transparency"? (57)
4. Why does the poem end with the speaker saying, "Touch me and you'll burn"? (57)

FOR FURTHER REFLECTION

1. Would you try to convince the speaker to stop dancing at the bar? How would you respond to her explanation of why she stays?
2. Is the kind of sexualized dancing the speaker is doing inherently exploitative to women?

Billy Collins (1941–) was born in New York City. He received a BA from the College of the Holy Cross in 1963 and went on to earn a PhD in English from the University of California, Riverside. He has written numerous books of poetry, including *The Art of Drowning* (1995), *Sailing Alone Around the Room* (2001), and *Picnic, Lightning* (1998), in which "Taking Off Emily Dickinson's Clothes" appears. Collins has won many awards including the Mark Twain Prize for Humor in Poetry. He was poet laureate of the United States from 2001 to 2003, and it was during that time that he created Poetry 180, a poetry website with 180 poems specially chosen for high school students. He has received fellowships from the National Endowment of the Arts and the Guggenheim Foundation and has taught English at Lehman College of the City of New York for many years.

Taking Off Emily Dickinson's Clothes

First, her tippet made of tulle,
easily lifted off her shoulders and laid
on the back of a wooden chair.

And her bonnet,
the bow undone with a light forward pull.

Then the long white dress, a more
complicated matter with mother-of-pearl
buttons down the back,
so tiny and numerous that it takes forever
before my hands can part the fabric,
like a swimmer's dividing water,
and slip inside.

You will want to know
that she was standing
by an open window in an upstairs bedroom,
motionless, a little wide-eyed,
looking out at the orchard below,
the white dress puddled at her feet
on the wide-board, hardwood floor.

The complexity of women's undergarments
in nineteenth-century America
is not to be waved off,
and I proceeded like a polar explorer
through clips, clasps, and moorings,

catches, straps, and whalebone stays,
sailing toward the iceberg of her nakedness.

Later, I wrote in a notebook
it was like riding a swan into the night,
but, of course, I cannot tell you everything—
the way she closed her eyes to the orchard,
how her hair tumbled free of its pins,
how there were sudden dashes
whenever we spoke.

What I can tell you is
it was terribly quiet in Amherst
that Sabbath afternoon,
nothing but a carriage passing the house,
a fly buzzing in a windowpane.

So I could plainly hear her inhale
when I undid the very top
hook-and-eye fastener of her corset

and I could hear her sigh when finally it was
unloosed,
the way some readers sigh when they realize
that Hope has feathers,
that reason is a plank,
that life is a loaded gun
that looks right at you with a yellow eye.

FOR DISCUSSION

1. Why does the speaker imagine undressing Emily Dickinson?
2. What does the speaker mean when he says, "The complexity of women's undergarments / in nineteenth-century America / is not to be waved off"? (61)
3. Why does the speaker explicitly address the reader and assume the reader wants to know the details of undressing Emily Dickinson? What does he mean when he says, "I cannot tell you everything"? (62)
4. In the final stanza of the poem, why does the speaker compare Emily Dickinson's sigh when her corset is unloosed to the sigh of readers of her poems?

FOR FURTHER REFLECTION

1. What is the tone of this poem? In what respects is it sexual, curious, aroused, or adoring?
2. What does Collins's poem say about the relation between the external characteristics of a writer's life and the meaning of a writer's works?

Joan Jacobs Brumberg (1944–) was born in Mount Vernon, New York. She received a BA from the University of Rochester and a PhD from the University of Virginia. Since 1979 she has taught courses in history, human development, and gender studies at Cornell University. In 1988 Brumberg published *Fasting Girls: The History of Anorexia Nervosa*, a groundbreaking study that brought to light the experiences of girls with eating disorders by citing more than one hundred diaries written as early as the 1830s. This book received multiple awards, including the Berkshire Book Prize and the John Hope Franklin Prize. Brumberg's research into body-image issues continued with the publication of *The Body Project: An Intimate History of American Girls* (1997), from which this selection is taken. She has received fellowships from the Guggenheim Foundation and the National Endowment for the Humanities.

Girl Advocacy Again
(selection)

At the end of the twentieth century, living in a girl's body is more complicated than it was a century ago. When the students in my seminar described how they managed the "bikini-line area," they were admitting, in a backhanded way, that their generation had taken on the burden of perfecting yet another body part. Their informed commentary on diet and exercise strategies, body sculpturing, liposuction, and mammoplasty all revealed that they had internalized the contemporary imperative for a perfect body, even as they stood apart from it and tried to understand it as a social and cultural phenomenon.

I was struck by the confusion they felt. On the one hand, their parents and teachers told them that being female was no bar to accomplishment. Yet girls of their generation learned from a very early age that the power of their gender was tied to what they looked like—and how "sexy" they were—rather than to character or achievement. Because of the visual images they had absorbed since they were toddlers, they invariably wanted to be thinner, a desire that motivated them to expend an enormous amount of time and energy controlling the appetite and working on their bodies, all the while thinking about food. Although they were aware that diet and exercise regimens could become obsessive and lead to eating disorders, in their own lives they walked a narrow line between the normal and the pathological. Almost all of them admitted that they did battle, on a daily basis, with what therapists in the eating disorders world call "bad body fever," a continuous internal commentary that constitutes a powerful form of self-punishment. "I'm gross," "My thighs are disgusting," "My stomach hangs out" are all typical refrains among the current generation, regardless of whether they are fat or thin. Marketers recognize these anxieties and play them to the hilt. For example, a 1990 advertisement for the popular hair product Dep simply assumed that girls did not like their bodies and that they worried about cellulite and saddlebag thighs.

My students were exquisitely sensitive to the cultural pressures surrounding them. They understood that their relationship to food and the body had been shaped by what they saw as little girls on television, at the movies, and in advertising. They were especially savvy in their analysis of marketing strategies, and adept in their ability to "deconstruct" messages about women in any ad, ranging from Oil of Olay to Calvin Klein to Jeep Cherokees. I really had little to teach them about what it means to live in a culture of unrelenting objectification where women's bodies are used to sell everything. Because of their age, and the nature of the developmental process, they already felt the pressure emanating from American popular culture, sometimes more acutely than I did.

But when it came to a historical understanding of their situation, they had little to say, except for a few naive claims about how much better things became for American women as a result of the demise of the corset and the emergence of more sexual freedom. Neither my students nor the many adult audiences to whom I have spoken since the publication in 1988 of my book on the history of anorexia nervosa really understood the historical process by which women exchanged external controls of the body for internal controls—or the ways in which the body became a central paradigm for the self in the twentieth century, thereby altering the experience of coming of age in some fundamental ways. This lack of attention to the historical roots of the "body problem" is what inspired me to write this book, and to articulate at its conclusion what is unique and dangerous about our present predicament.

Contemporary girls are in trouble because we are experiencing a mismatch between biology and culture. At this moment in our history, young women develop physically earlier than ever before, but they do so within a society that does not protect or nurture them in ways that were once a hallmark of American life. Instead of supporting our early-maturing girls, or offering them some special relief or protection from the unrelenting self-scrutiny that the marketplace and modern media both thrive on, contemporary culture exacerbates normal adolescent self-consciousness and encourages precocious sexuality. Too often popular culture and peer groups, rather than parents or other responsible adults, call the cadence in contemporary teenage life. Contemporary girls *seem* to have more autonomy, but their freedom is laced with peril. Despite sophisticated packaging, many remain emotionally immature, and that makes it all the more difficult to withstand the sexually brutal and commercially rapacious society in which they grow up.

The current vulnerability of American girls is linked to the decline of the Victorian "protective umbrella" that sheltered and nurtured them well into the twentieth century. Victorian society could be repressive and unkind, and many mothers failed their daughters by not talking about normal physiological functions, but girls today are failed in a different way. On the basis of what we know from their diaries, there has been a curious decline in maternal involvement and supervision of girls over the past century. Although middle-class parents are invested more than ever before in the health and education of their adolescent girls, one of the most intimate aspects of the mother-daughter relationship—menarche and menstruation—had been relegated to medicine and to the marketplace by the time of World War II. After the war, there were also important economic changes that led to a broad retreat from girls and their social needs: more mothers had to work outside the home, so they had fewer hours to volunteer in community and church groups for young women. At the same time, nuclear family life also became more private and more isolated. By the 1950s, a married woman's primary allegiance was to her own children, not to those of others. Today, sustained involvement with girls other than one's own daughters is unusual in the world of middle-class women, unless these relationships are structured by their professional responsibilities as teachers and professors, nurses and doctors, nutritionists, psychologists, and social workers.

We also think about equality differently, and that has had an impact on how we handle adolescent girls and issues of sexuality. Beginning in the late 1960s and 1970s, the traditional notion that women need special protections because of their biology was discredited. In 1972, Congress passed the influential Title IX legislation, which made it illegal to discriminate on the basis of sex in most aspects of American life. This long-awaited gain, which opened up new areas of education, employment, and sports, meant that efforts to protect and nurture girls in special ways now seemed old-fashioned, if not reactionary. In the interest of fairness, feminists like myself wanted no part of any educational program or organization that treated adolescent girls differently from boys. This was an understandable reaction to the "ovarian determinism" that used biology to rationalize female inequality. We agitated for the abolition of discriminatory, old-fashioned rules that required curfews for girls but not boys because we wanted our daughters to have the same social and sexual equality that we demanded for ourselves. We also were willing to relent on statutory rape laws, a favorite cause of Progressive reformers who struggled to protect the innate "virtue" of girls from the well-known "vices" of men by raising the age of consent from ten and twelve to eighteen or twenty. As columnist Ellen Goodman rightly points out, our desire to overturn the "double standard" of sexuality allowed us to put these laws into "mothballs" and transformed adolescent girls from "jailbait" into "fair game."

In the effort to be different from our staid and sometimes repressive mothers and fathers, many of us also changed the ways in which we parent. According to Tufts University psychologist David Elkind, our current postmodern style of family nurturance pays little deference to the old ideal of protecting children from life's vicissitudes or adult knowledge. Today's "harried parents" expect their "hurried children" to be autonomous, competent, and sophisticated by the time they are adolescents. This pseudosophistication leads adults to abandon the traditional position of setting limits and forming values, particularly in matters of sex, that characterized previous generations of parents, teachers, and female mentors. Adolescents raised in this permissive environment become extremely stressed precisely because they have been denied a comfortable envelope of adult values that allows them time to adjust emotionally to their developing bodies and new social roles. This situation is made even more troublesome by the fact that we do not prepare girls adequately for the range of sexual choices existing in the United States in the 1990s. Instead, they absorb a great deal of erroneous information from popular culture (the "entertainment" model of sex education) or they are lectured about the virtues of abstinence (the "Just say no" model).

As a society, we edged down the road of sexual liberalism without giving much thought to the situation of girls or to changing historical circumstances. What no one could foresee in the 1970s was the way in which early sexual maturation, our commitment to adolescent sexual expression, and the HIV virus would all coincide within the next two decades. In the 1990s, adolescent sexuality is more dangerous than ever before because the players are so young and the disease environment is so deadly. And the peril in this biological state of affairs is heightened by our social arrangements and our televisual environment. We have backed off from traditional supervision or guidance of adolescent girls; yet we sustain a popular culture that is permeated by sexual imagery, so much so that many young women regard their bodies and sexual allure as the primary currency of the realm.

Many different kinds of social critics now agree that American girls make the trip from menarche into adulthood without either knowledgeable guides or appropriate protective gear. For that reason, we may want to borrow at least one operating principle from our Victorian ancestors and consider the idea that young women deserve to be eased into womanhood more slowly than is the case today. In the 1990s, though, we cannot buy time with silence, the way Victorian mothers did. Contemporary girls need to be educated about the worst excesses of a society saturated with sex, such as the popular notion that violence is "sexy," or that the capacity for instant "intimacy" is a desirable personal characteristic. While contemporary girls enjoy many expressive freedoms that older women were denied when they were young, there is growing evidence that sexuality can be extremely dangerous when there is no system of responsible adult nurturance or guidance. From a historian's perspective, our timing has been off: as a society, we discarded the Victorian moral umbrella over girls before we agreed upon useful strategies and programs—a kind of "social Gore-Tex"—to help them stay dry. We live now with the consequences. . . .

Many people think that the answer to our problems with girls is simply to turn the clock back. Some folks plainly liked it better when the hymen was the Maginot Line of virginity and young women were punished for even minor breaches of feminine decorum. Admittedly, there are enormous risks for adolescent girls in the contemporary world, but this is not sufficient cause to turn the clock back to an era when it was acceptable to treat women as though they were asexual objects living in divinely inspired subordination to men. Besides, it's impossible. There have been too many deep changes in our economic and social life, changes that are irrevocable now that they are embedded in our daily lives as well as our minds. Although we can learn from the past, at the end of the twentieth century we need to fashion a new strategy of girl advocacy that acknowledges the convergence of earlier sexual maturation with our current cultural imperatives.

One of the first things we need to clarify is what it means to be an adolescent girl in a sexually permissive society. If you are not convinced that our culture has been sexualized, spend a morning at home watching the most popular talk shows and see how often sexual behavior, and explicit talk about sexual acts and sexual orientation, is the focus of discussion. Then watch some prime-time television at night, and count the number of times sexual innuendo, sex acts, and sexual violence are central to both comedy and drama. Growing up in this kind of environment is vastly different from what it was like to grow up a century ago, when middle-class girls like Lou Henry lived securely in a culture of modesty, the product of a high level of sexual repression. But it is also distinctly different from what many of us experienced even as late as the 1960s, when things really began to "loosen up." Today, the standard of modesty and decorum is extremely low, at least on television, and that fact has profound implications for how adolescents handle their bodies, regardless of gender. Our contemporary immodesty, however, is more problematic for girls, because it is their bodies, not the bodies of boys, that are consistently evaluated, displayed, and brutalized. Because we no longer maintain any special structural or ideological protections for them, many adolescent girls are alone and unattended in this environment as they struggle to make sense of their own sexuality and what it means to be an adult woman.

As long as there is no special support system for girls, life in a sexually permissive society is both confusing and dangerous for adolescents. This is a hard fact for many of us to admit, given our commitment to sexual expression. But facing the hard reality of HIV, we probably need, at least, to refine our idea that sexual activity in adolescence is inevitable and intrinsically worthwhile. In fact, right now, a totally permissive attitude may be as unthinking as the reactionary approach that preaches a rigid return to Victorian standards of virginity. In the university town where I live, I often hear the "pro sex" argument, usually from feminists like myself. Many of my friends maintain that sexual expression is as important an American right as those guaranteed in the Bill of Rights and the Constitution. In this view, adolescent girls should be totally autonomous in their sexual decision making; by contrast, among conservatives, adolescent sexuality is a matter for firm parental control.

As a historian with a long-standing interest in developmental psychology, I question both approaches because they ignore the relevance of age, and the ways in which popular culture has evolved in the past thirty years. Although I applaud the social freedom and economic opportunities enjoyed by the current cohort of high school and college girls, their "autonomy" seems to me to be oversold, if not illusory. Many young women, particularly those under twenty, do not have the emotional resources to be truly autonomous or to withstand outside pressures from peers and boyfriends, whom they desperately want to please. They are also locked into a commercially driven television culture that exploits female bodies in unprecedented and, increasingly, violent ways. By their own admission, this environment of slick images and quick seductions shapes their desires, and their sense of self, even if they try to resist. As we consider ways to respond to the predicament of our girls, we need to acknowledge these facts: teen-agers do not always understand their own self-interest. And real autonomy may be impossible in a society where adolescents' expectations and desires are determined so consistently by media and advertising. How can we expect adolescent girls to be in charge of their sexuality when adult women are still struggling for equality in this domain?

Given what we know about the deep commercial investment in girls' bodies, and also the tenor of our contemporary culture, it seems unrealistic to think that young girls can operate independently, without parental or adult assistance, or that they should be expected to. Like Carol Gilligan, I think that most girls desire and profit from connection with their mothers, their aunts, their women teachers, and even their friends, and that individual autonomy has been oversold as a model for female development and for social life in general. Because of what we know about girls, and the ways in which the failure to set limits leaves them dangerously afloat, I am no longer quiet around ideologues who make sexual freedom and autonomy the ultimate value for adolescent girls. While they are still in their teens, there are other freedoms from which girls would profit even more, such as the freedom to be heard at school in an equal way with boys, or the freedom to develop their bodies without constantly measuring themselves against some artificial, airbrushed ideal. These would help girls overcome the well-known "confidence gap" that not only stymies their performance in life but also leads them into sexual liaisons where there is little equality or pleasure.

As we prepare girls for life in the twenty-first century, we need to initiate a larger multigenerational dialogue that speaks to the reality of earlier maturation, the need for sexual expression, and the nature of contemporary culture. These discussions must offer more than such simplistic axioms as "Just say no," and more than logistical instruction about how to hold off male advances or practice safe sex. Whether at home or at school, our discussions need to be responsive to the developmental needs of girls, needs generated by their biological and emotional growth as well as the popular culture in which they live. This is the terrain on which liberals and feminists should do battle with the forces of reaction. Although many people will not like it, American girls should be presented, as they mature, with the full range of sexual options that young women now experience, including lesbianism as well as heterosexuality, and also thoughtful discussions of female pleasure as well as danger. In the teen years, the focus should not be on finalizing a clear-cut sexual identity—Are you straight or are you gay?—but on helping young women evolve a standard of sexual ethics that has integrity, regardless of the gender of their partners.

Sexual ethics—that is, a coherent philosophy about what is fair and equitable in the realm of the intimate—is what girls need in a society that treats women's bodies in a sexually brutal and commercially rapacious way. Instead of "shock talk" television, the vehicle Americans now use to explore the most lurid, flamboyant side of the sexual revolution, female professionals—particularly social workers, psychologists, nurses, doctors, and teachers like myself—need to create a national forum for developing a code of sexual ethics for adolescent girls in a postvirginal age. This discussion will not be easy, but I think most Americans can agree on at least two things: the discussion must include girls themselves, and the goals should be safety, reciprocity, and responsibility in all forms of human intimacy.

Sexual intercourse during the high school years is dangerous—most Americans would agree on that—but we will never be able to restrict it legally, by age, the way we restrict other adult privileges such as driving and drinking. One way to curb sexual activity is to make it harder for young people to be alone in seductive situations—by imposing rules and curfews, for example—but even this kind of control can backfire, since some teenagers make "breaking rules" an end in and of itself. In a society like ours, where teenagers of both sexes have an unprecedented amount of social freedom, traditional mechanisms of social control are hard to reinstitute and also inadequate to the job. While they are still in their early and middle teens, adolescent girls may find comfort in sensible parental constraints, such as curfews, but they will ultimately need something more than rules to help them navigate a successful passage into adulthood. What they need is a code of personal ethics that helps them make sense of their own emotions, as well as the social pressures that are part of the postvirginal world.

For parents, sexual ethics means facing up to our responsibilities to nurture and protect our young, even if it means that we must take an unfashionable stand against the vulgarity of popular culture and the power of adolescent peer groups. Although knowledge is always preferable to misinformation, we need to recognize that simply providing clear-cut, visually interesting materials about contraception or "safe sex" is not the same as helping young women develop a sense of what is a fair, pleasurable, and responsible use of their bodies. Freedom of information helps, but it does not always lead to healthy decision making, especially in the realm of youthful female sexuality. Adolescent girls simply are not mature enough, or sufficiently in control of their lives, to resist all the social and commercial pressures they face in our hypersexual, televisual environment. For that reason, I think there are plenty of "values" that sensible liberal people can agree upon without allowing conservative ideologues to act as if they have a monopoly in the "moral values" business. For example, responsibility means not having kids unless you are prepared to support them emotionally and economically.

But before we try to initiate this critical discussion about sexual ethics for girls, we need to acknowledge something critical about their experience. As long as they feel so unhappy with their bodies, it is unlikely that they can achieve the sexual agency that they need for complete and successful lives in the contemporary world. Girls who do not feel good about themselves need the affirmation of others, and that need, unfortunately, almost always empowers male desire. In other words, girls who hate their bodies do not make good decisions about partners, or about the kind of sexual activity that is in their best interest. Because they want to be wanted so much, they are susceptible to manipulation, to flattery, even to abuse. Body angst is not only a boost to commerce, as this book has shown; it makes the worst forms of sexual flattery acceptable, which explains why some girls feel ambivalent about sexual harassment and do not know how to respond.

I am not the first person to make a link between girls' bodies and cultural values. Even before Elizabeth Cady Stanton broached the subject in her famous lecture "Our Girls," there were other Americans who understood this critical connection. In 1871, in a book that was called *Our Girls*, a Boston physician and health reformer named Dioclesian Lewis argued that America's adolescent girls needed to develop greater confidence in their bodies in order to become effective students, teachers, and mothers. In this popular book, and also on the lecture circuit, Dr. Lewis tried to redirect young girls away from idle pursuits (such as piano playing and French lessons) and fashions (such as tight lacing and narrow shoes), because he believed that these interests encouraged indolence and fragility. Lewis, like Stanton, was more than just an opponent of the corset; he was an advocate for girls, and his enthusiasm for their potential was boundless. "My hopes of the future rest upon the girls," Lewis wrote optimistically. "My patriotism clings to the girls. I believe America's future pivots on this great woman revolution."

Although the forms of girl advocacy change over time—in the 1990s we uphold rights to personal freedom and expression that were unthinkable in the 1870s—we need to consider being "girl advocates" again. For this reason, I admire the style of both Stanton and Lewis, and I also support the traditional idea of collective responsibility implied by the words "our girls." In the 1990s, we need to make an investment in *all* American girls, not just our own middle-class daughters.

The hope of Stanton and Lewis that America's adolescent girls would put aside trivial body projects for more creative and meaningful pursuits has not, unfortunately, been realized. Neither the outspoken feminist nor the eccentric doctor could foresee that as American women shed their corsets, they would adjust their waistlines to a different set of expectations and constraints that would be even harder and tougher than cotton laces and whalebone stays. Over the course of the twentieth century, girls' bodies have been a critical index of our social and economic life, in ways that we are just beginning to understand. The rise of scientific medicine, the decline of parental and community supervision, the triumph of a visual consumer culture, and the changing nature of intimacy in our society are all encoded in their youthful flesh, and in the social problems they now face. Although evolution in fashion is part of this story, there is more at stake here than simply changing hemlines or bustlines.

In reality, there is an interaction between biology and culture that is shaping the experience of contemporary girls in some critical and troublesome ways. More than any other group in the population, girls and their bodies have borne the brunt of twentieth-century social change, and we ignore that fact at our peril. It is time for us to talk—squarely and fairly—about the ways in which American girlhood has changed and what girls must have to ensure a safe and creative future.

FOR DISCUSSION

1. Why does Brumberg believe it is important to understand "the historical process by which women exchanged external controls of the body for internal controls"? (66–67)
2. Why does Brumberg consider the autonomy of high school and college girls to be "oversold, if not illusory"? (73)
3. In Brumberg's view, why is it essential for adults to help adolescent girls and young women develop "a standard of sexual ethics"? (75) Why does she see women as more vulnerable than men in this respect?
4. Why does Brumberg believe that girls will have trouble achieving "sexual agency" if they are "unhappy with their bodies"? (76)

FOR FURTHER REFLECTION

1. Do you agree with Brumberg's statement that women still tend to be judged by how "sexy" they are rather than by their character or achievement?
2. Since 1997, when *The Body Project* (the source of this selection) was published, do you think that things have gotten better or worse for adolescent girls and young women? Do you agree with Brumberg that society should do more to protect and help young women and adolescent girls with their body image problems?

Mark Doty (1953–) grew up the son of an army engineer and lived in various communities across the United States. He received a BA from Drake University and an MFA in creative writing from Goddard College. He has written numerous books of poetry and three memoirs. Doty is the winner of the 2008 National Book Award for his collection *Fire to Fire: New and Selected Poems*. He has taught creative writing at a number of colleges and universities and has been awarded fellowships from the Guggenheim Foundation and the National Endowment for the Arts. "Esta Noche" was first published in *My Alexandria: Poems* (1993), written in part as a response to his partner's illness and death from AIDS. The collection won Britain's T. S. Eliot Award—making Doty the only American to have been so honored.

Esta Noche

In a dress with a black tulip's sheen
    la fabulosa Lola enters, late, mounts the stairs
to the plywood platform, and begs whoever runs
    the wobbling spot to turn the lights down

to something flattering. When they halo her
    with a petal-toned gel, she sets to haranguing,
shifting in and out of two languages like gowns
    or genders to *please* have a little respect

for the girls, flashing the one entrancing
    and unavoidable gap in the center of her upper teeth.
And when the cellophane drop goes black,
    a new spot coronas her in a wig

fit for the end of a century,
    and she tosses back her hair—risky gesture—
and raises her arms like a widow in a blood tragedy,
    all will and black lace, and lip-syncs "You and Me

against the World." She's a man
    you wouldn't look twice at in street clothes,
two hundred pounds of hard living, the gap in her smile
    sadly narrative—but she's a monument,

in the mysterious permission of the dress.
    This is Esta Noche, a Latin drag bar in the Mission,
its black door a gap in the face
    of a battered wall. All over the neighborhood

storefront windows show all night
    shrined hats and gloves, wedding dresses,
First Communion's frothing lace:
    gowns of perfection and commencement,

fixed promises glowing. In the dress
    the color of the spaces between streetlamps
Lola stands unassailable, the dress
    in which she is in the largest sense

fabulous: a lesson, a criticism and colossus
    of gender, all fire and irony. Her spine's
perfectly erect, only her fluid hands moving
    and her head turned slightly to one side.

She hosts the pageant, Wednesdays and Saturdays,
    and men come in from the streets, the trains,
and the repair shops, lean together to rank
    the artifice of the awkward or lovely

Lola welcomes onto the stage: Victoria, Elena,
    Francie, lamé pumps and stockings and always
the rippling night pulled down over broad shoulders
    and flounced around the hips, liquid,

the black silk of esta noche
    proving that perfection and beauty are so alien
they almost never touch. Tonight, she says,
    put it on. The costume is license

and calling. She says you could wear the whole damn
    black sky and all its spangles. It's the only night
we have to stand on. Put it on,
    it's the only thing we have to wear.

FOR DISCUSSION

1. Why does Lola ask that the stage lights be more flattering and that the audience "*please* have a little respect / for the girls"? (81) Why are the details of the performance and its reception so important to Lola?
2. Why does the speaker not reveal that Lola is a man until the fifth stanza?
3. What does it mean that Lola is "a lesson, a criticism and colossus / of gender"? (82)
4. How does "the black silk of esta noche" prove "that perfection and beauty are so alien / they almost never touch"? (82) At the end of the poem, why does Lola say that the black sky is "the only thing we have to wear"? (83)

FOR FURTHER REFLECTION

1. Are the performances of female impersonators more likely to serve as criticisms or endorsements of traditional feminine roles and mannerisms?
2. Why might Lola choose "You and Me Against the World" to lip-sync? What other songs might she sing, and why?

Susan Minot (1956–) was raised in Manchester, Massachusetts. She graduated from Brown University and received an MFA from Columbia University in New York City. Her first novel, *Monkeys*, was published in 1986 and became a national bestseller. It tells the story of a large upper-class family and is based, in part, on Minot's own experiences growing up as one of seven siblings. She collaborated with director Bernardo Bertolucci to create the screenplay for the movie *Stealing Beauty* (1996), and she cowrote the screenplay for the movie *Evening* (2007), which is based on her 1999 novel of the same name. Much of Minot's work focuses on how women interact with lovers, friends, family, and themselves. Her story "Lust" is from the collection *Lust and Other Stories* (1989).

Lust

Leo was from a long time ago, the first one I ever saw nude. In the spring before the Hellmans filled their pool, we'd go down there in the deep end, with baby oil, and like that. I met him the first month away at boarding school. He had a halo from the campus light behind him. I flipped.

Roger was fast. In his illegal car, we drove to the reservoir, the radio blaring, talking fast, fast, fast. He was always going for my zipper. He got kicked out sophomore year.

By the time the band got around to playing "Wild Horses," I had tasted Bruce's tongue. We were clicking in the shadows on the other side of the amplifier, out of Mrs. Donovan's line of vision. It tasted like salt, with my neck bent back, because we had been dancing so hard before.

Tim's line: "I'd like to see you in a bathing suit." I knew it was his line when he said the exact same thing to Annie Hines.

You'd go on walks to get off campus. It was raining like hell, my sweater as sopped as a wet sheep. Tim pinned me to a tree, the woods light brown and dark brown, a white house half hidden with the lights already on. The water was as loud as a crowd hissing. He made certain comments about my forehead, about my cheeks.

We started off sitting at one end of the couch and then our feet were squished against the armrest and then he went over to turn off the TV and came back after he had taken off his shirt and then we slid onto the floor and he got up again to close the door, then came back to me, a body waiting on the rug.

You'd try to wipe off the table or to do the dishes and Willie would untuck your shirt and get his hands up under in front, standing behind you, making puffy noises in your ear.

He likes it when I wash my hair. He covers his face with it and if I start to say something, he goes, "Shush."

For a long time, I had Philip on the brain. The less they noticed you, the more you got them on the brain.

My parents had no idea. Parents never really know what's going on, especially when you're away at school most of the time. If she met them, my mother might say, "Oliver seems nice" or "I like that one" without much of an opinion. If she didn't like them, "He's a funny fellow, isn't he?" or "Johnny's perfectly nice but a drink of water." My father was too shy to talk to them at all unless they played sports and he'd ask them about that.

The sand was almost cold underneath because the sun was long gone. Eben piled a mound over my feet, patting around my ankles, the ghostly surf rumbling behind him in the dark. He was the first person I ever knew who died, later that summer, in a car crash. I thought about it for a long time.

"Come here," he says on the porch.

I go over to the hammock and he takes my wrist with two fingers.

"What?"

He kisses my palm then directs my hand to his fly.

Songs went with whichever boy it was. "Sugar Magnolia" was Tim, with the line "Rolling in the rushes / down by the riverside." With "Darkness, Darkness," I'd picture Philip with his long hair. Hearing "Under My Thumb" there'd be the smell of Jamie's suede jacket.

We hid in the listening rooms during study hall. With a record cover over the door's window, the teacher on duty couldn't look in. I came out flushed and heady and back at the dorm was surprised how red my lips were in the mirror.

One weekend at Simon's brother's, we stayed inside all day with the shades down, in bed, then went out to Store 24 to get some ice cream. He stood at the magazine rack and read through *Mad* while I got butterscotch sauce, craving something sweet.

I could do some things well. Some things I was good at, like math or painting or even sports, but the second a boy put his arm around me, I forgot about wanting to do anything else, which felt like a relief at first until it became like sinking into a muck.

It was different for a girl.

. . .

When we were little, the brothers next door tied up our ankles. They held the door of the goat house and wouldn't let us out till we showed them our underpants. Then they'd forget about being after us and when we played whiffle ball, I'd be just as good as they were.

Then it got to be different. Just because you have on a short skirt, they yell from the cars, slowing down for a while, and if you don't look, they screech off and call you a bitch.

"What's the matter with me?" they say, point-blank.

Or else, "Why won't you go out with me? I'm not asking you to get married," about to get mad.

Or it'd be, trying to be reasonable, in a regular voice, "Listen, I just want to have a good time."

So I'd go because I couldn't think of something to say back that wouldn't be obvious, and if you go out with them, you sort of have to do something.

I sat between Mack and Eddie in the front seat of the pickup. They were having a fight about something. I've a feeling about me.

Certain nights you'd feel a certain surrender, maybe if you'd had wine. The surrender would be forgetting yourself and you'd put your nose to his neck and feel like a squirrel, safe, at rest, in a restful dream. But then you'd start to slip from that and the dark would come in and there'd be a cave. You make out the dim shape of the windows and feel yourself become a cave, filled absolutely with air, or with a sadness that wouldn't stop.

. . .

Teenage years. You know just what you're doing and don't see the things that start to get in the way

Lots of boys, but never two at the same time. One was plenty to keep you in a state. You'd start to see a boy and something would rush over you like a fast storm cloud and you couldn't possibly think of anyone else. Boys took it differently. Their eyes perked up at any little number that walked by. You'd act like you weren't noticing.

The joke was that the school doctor gave out the pill like aspirin. He didn't ask you anything. I was fifteen. We had a picture of him in assembly, holding up an IUD shaped like a T. Most girls were on the pill, if anything, because they couldn't handle a diaphragm. I kept the dial in my top drawer like my mother and thought of her each time I tipped out the yellow tablets in the morning before chapel.

If they were too shy, I'd be more so. Andrew was nervous. We stayed up with his family album, sharing a pack of Old Golds. Before it got light, we turned on the TV. A man was explaining how to plant seedlings. His mouth jerked to the side in a tic. Andrew thought it was a riot and kept imitating him. I laughed to be polite. When we finally dozed off, he dared to put his arm around me, but that was it.

You wait till they come to you. With half fright, half swagger, they stand one step down. They dare to touch the button on your coat then lose their nerve and quickly drop their hand so you—you'd do anything for them. You touch their cheek.

. . .

The girls sit around in the common room and talk about boys, smoking their heads off.

"What are you complaining about?" says Jill to me when we talk about problems.

"Yeah," says Giddy. "You always have a boyfriend."

I look at them and think, As if.

I thought the worst thing anyone could call you was a cockteaser. So, if you flirted, you had to be prepared to go through with it. Sleeping with someone was perfectly normal once you had done it. You didn't really worry about it. But there were other problems. The problems had to do with something else entirely.

Mack was during the hottest summer ever recorded. We were renting a house on an island with all sorts of other people. No one slept during the heat wave, walking around the house with nothing on, which we were used to because of the nude beach. In the living room, Eddie lay on top of a coffee table to cool off. Mack and I, with the bedroom door open for air, sweated and sweated all night.

"I can't take this," he said at 3:00 a.m. "I'm going for a swim." He and some guys down the hall went to the beach. The heat put me on edge. I sat on a cracked chest by the open window and smoked and smoked till I felt even worse, waiting for something—I guess for him to get back.

One was on a camping trip in Colorado. We zipped our sleeping bags together, the coyotes' hysterical chatter far away. Other couples murmured in other tents. Paul was up before sunrise, starting a fire for breakfast. He wasn't much of a talker in the daytime. At night, his hand leafed about in the hair at my neck.

There'd be times when you overdid it. You'd get carried away. All the next day, you'd be in a total fog, delirious, absent-minded, crossing the street and nearly getting run over.

The more girls a boy has, the better. He has a bright look, having reaped fruits, blooming. He stalks around, sure-shouldered, and you have the feeling he's got more in him, a fatter heart, more stories to tell. For a girl, with each boy it's as though a petal gets plucked each time.

Then you start to get tired. You begin to feel diluted, like watered-down stew.

Oliver came skiing with us. We lolled by the fire after everyone had gone to bed. Each creak you'd think was someone coming downstairs. The silver loop bracelet he gave me had been a present from his girlfriend before.

On vacations, we went skiing, or you'd go south if someone invited you. Some people had apartments in New York that their families hardly ever used. Or summer houses, or older sisters. We always managed to find someplace to go.

We made the plan at coffee hour. Simon snuck out and met me at Main Gate after lights out. We crept to the chapel and spent the night in the balcony. He tasted like onions from a submarine sandwich.

The boys are one of two ways: either they can't sit still or they don't move. In front of the TV, they won't budge. On weekends they play touch football while we sit on the sidelines, picking blades of grass to chew on, and watch. We're always watching them run around. We shiver in the stands, knocking our boots together to keep our toes warm, and they whizz across the ice, chopping their sticks around the puck. When they're in the rink, they refuse to look at you, only eyeing each other beneath low helmets. You cheer for them but they don't look up, even if it's a face-off when nothing's happening, even if they're doing drills before any game has started at all.

Dancing under the pink tent, he bent down and whispered in my ear. We slipped away to the lawn on the other side of the hedge. Much later, as he was leaving the buffet with two plates of eggs and sausage, I saw the grass stains on the knees of his white pants.

Tim's was shaped like a banana, with a graceful curve to it. They're all different. Willie's like a bunch of walnuts when nothing was happening, another's as thin as a thin hot dog. But it's like faces; you're never really surprised.

Still, you're not sure what to expect.

I look into his face and he looks back. I look into his eyes and they look back at mine. Then they look down at my mouth so I look at his mouth, then back to his eyes then, backing up, at his whole face. I think, Who? Who are you? His head tilts to one side.

I say, "Who are you?"

"What do you mean?"

"Nothing."

I look at his eyes again, deeper. Can't tell who he is, what he thinks.

"What?" he says. I look at his mouth.

"I'm just wondering," I say and go wandering across his face. Study the chin line. It's shaped like a persimmon.

"Who are you? What are you thinking?"
He says, "What the hell are you talking about?"

Then they get mad after, when you say enough is enough. After, when it's easier to explain that you don't want to. You wouldn't dream of saying that maybe you weren't really ready to in the first place.

Gentle Eddie. We waded into the sea, the waves round and plowing in, buffalo-headed, slapping our thighs. I put my arms around his freckled shoulders and he held me up, buoyed by the water, and rocked me like a seashell.

I had no idea whose party it was, the apartment jam-packed, stepping over people in the hallway. The room with the music was practically empty, the bare floor, me in red shoes. This fellow slides onto one knee and takes me around the waist and we rock to jazzy tunes, with my toes pointing heavenward, and waltz and spin and dip to "Smoke Gets in Your Eyes" or "I'll Love You Just for Now." He puts his head to my chest, runs a sweeping hand down my inside thigh and we go loose-limbed and sultry and as smooth as silk and I stamp my red heels and he takes me into a swoon. I never saw him again after that but I thought, I could have loved that one.

You wonder how long you can keep it up. You begin to feel as if you're showing through, like a bathroom window that only lets in grey light, the kind you can't see out of.

They keep coming around. Johnny drives up at Easter vacation from Baltimore and I let him in the kitchen with everyone sound asleep. He has friends waiting in the car.

"What are you, crazy? It's pouring out there," I say.

"It's okay," he says. "They understand."

So he gets some long kisses from me, against the refrigerator, before he goes because I hate those girls who push away a boy's face as if she were made out of Ivory soap, as if she's that much greater than he is.

The note on my cubby told me to see the headmaster. I had no idea for what. He had received complaints about my amorous displays on the town green. It was Willie that spring. The headmaster told me he didn't care what I did but that Casey Academy had a reputation to uphold in the town. He lowered his glasses on his nose. "We've got twenty acres of woods on this campus," he said. "If you want to smooch with your boyfriend, there are twenty acres for you to do it out of the public eye. You read me?"

Everybody'd get weekend permissions for different places, then we'd all go to someone's house whose parents were away. Usually there'd be more boys than girls. We raided the liquor closet and smoked pot at the kitchen table and you'd never know who would end up where, or with whom. There were always disasters. Ceci got bombed and cracked her head open on the banister and needed stitches. Then there was the time Wendel Blair walked through the picture window at the Lowes' and got slashed to ribbons.

He scared me. In bed, I didn't dare look at him. I lay back with my eyes closed, luxuriating because he knew all sorts of expert angles, his hands never fumbling, going over my whole body, pressing the hair up and off the back of my head, giving an extra hip shove, as if to say *There.* I parted my eyes slightly, keeping the screen of my lashes low because it was too much to look at him, his mouth loose and pink and parted, his eyes looking through my forehead, or kneeling up, looking through my throat. I was ashamed but couldn't look him in the eye.

You wonder about things feeling a little off-kilter. You begin to feel like a piece of pounded veal.

At boarding school, everyone gets depressed. We go in and see the housemother, Mrs. Gunther. She got married when she was eighteen. Mr. Gunther was her high school sweetheart, the only boyfriend she ever had.

"And you knew you wanted to marry him right off?" we ask her.

She smiles and says, "Yes."

"They always want something from you," says Jill, complaining about her boyfriend.

"Yeah," says Giddy. "You always feel like you have to deliver something."

"You do," says Mrs. Gunther. "Babies."

After sex, you curl up like a shrimp, something deep inside you ruined, slammed in a place that sickens at slamming, and slowly you fill up with an overwhelming sadness, an elusive gaping worry. You don't try to explain it, filled with the knowledge that it's nothing after all, everything filling up finally and absolutely with death. After the briskness of loving, loving stops. And you roll over with death stretched out alongside you like a feather boa, or a snake, light as air, and you . . . you don't even ask for anything or try to say something to him because it's obviously your own damn fault. You haven't been able to—to what? To open your heart. You open your legs but can't, or don't dare anymore, to open your heart.

• • •

It starts this way:

You stare into their eyes. They flash like all the stars are out. They look at you seriously, their eyes at a low burn and their hands no matter what starting off shy and with such a gentle touch that the only thing you can do is take that tenderness and let yourself be swept away. When, with one attentive finger they tuck the hair behind your ear, you—

You do everything they want.

Then comes after. After when they don't look at you. They scratch their balls, stare at the ceiling. Or if they do turn, their gaze is altogether changed. They are surprised. They turn casually to look at you, distracted, and get a mild distracted surprise. You're gone. Their blank look tells you that the girl they were fucking is not there anymore. You seem to have disappeared.

FOR DISCUSSION

1. Why does the narrator choose to enumerate the boys, as if they are being read off a list or from the pages of a diary?
2. What does the narrator mean when she says, "The less they noticed you, the more you got them on the brain"? (88)
3. After sex, why does the narrator begin to imagine death stretched out alongside her "like a feather boa, or a snake"? (97)
4. What does the narrator mean when she says that "you don't even ask for anything or try to say something to him because it's obviously your own damn fault"? (97)

FOR FURTHER REFLECTION

1. Does Minot's story suggest that sex should be an end in itself, or that it serves as a pathway to other kinds of powerful connections between people?
2. Do you agree that "the more girls a boy has, the better. . . . For a girl, with each boy it's as though a petal gets plucked each time"? (93)

Louann Brizendine (1952–) is a practicing psychiatrist and professor of clinical psychiatry. She received a BA in neurobiology from the University of California, Berkeley and studied medicine at Yale, completing her residency in psychiatry at Harvard. She served on Harvard's psychiatry faculty for several years before joining the faculty of the University of California, San Francisco's medical school. In 1994 Brizendine founded the UCSF Women's Mood and Hormone Clinic, which, according to its website, "is a unique psychiatric clinic designed to assess and treat women of all ages experiencing disruption of mood, energy, anxiety, sexual function and well-being due to hormonal influences on the brain." "Love and Trust" is an excerpt from her first book, *The Female Brain* (2006), which was translated into twenty-six languages. Brizendine also wrote *The Male Brain*, published in 2010.

Love and Trust

Melissa, a brassy San Francisco film producer, really wanted to fall in love. Her career was finally chugging along at a steady pace, and at age thirty-two, she was ready to move into the next phase of her life. She now wanted a family and the continuity of a relationship with a man who would stick by her for more than a few sexually charged months. The only problem was that she couldn't seem to connect with the right one. She would go on countless dates through setups, or with men she met on the Internet, but none was touching off the flurry of butterflies in her stomach or that intense, irrational need to be around him all the time.

One night her best friend, Leslie, called and asked Melissa to go salsa dancing. But Melissa wasn't in the mood. She wanted to stay home, relax, and watch TV, but Leslie was relentless, so Melissa acquiesced. She tousled her curly hair to look sexy, put on a swirly skirt, her new red suede heels, and bee-sting red lipstick, which made her mouth pop out. She grabbed a taxi over to the dance club.

Leslie was already inside drinking a margarita when Melissa arrived. As they were getting loose to hit the dance floor, Melissa saw a tall, handsome man with a sculpted face, olive skin, and a shock of nearly black hair across the room. "Wow, he's gorgeous," she said.

She turned back to Leslie and whispered for her to glance over at the man, but it was too late. He was already walking toward them. Melissa was locked in gaze with this stranger. A wave of energy shot up her back. It was the feeling she hadn't experienced in all the months of her bad dates. There was something vaguely familiar about him. "Hmm, who *is* that?" she whispered under her breath to Leslie, as her brain's cortex scanned her memory banks. No match was found, but all her attention circuits were now on "mating alert status." Is he here alone or with someone? she wondered. She looked around for one of the gorgeous women who always seem to be attached to these perfect-looking guys but saw no one. And he was still walking toward her.

The closer he got, the more unfocused Melissa became on her friend's story. She grabbed her drink tightly. Her eyes and attention were riveted on him, taking in every detail—his leather Armani shoes, his sexy black cords, and no wedding ring on his left finger. Everything else dropped into the background as her brain honed to make contact. She felt like she was falling in love. The mating impulse had taken over.

"Hi, I'm Rob," he said, leaning against the bar nervously. His voice was pure velvet. "Have we met before?" Melissa was unable to hear his words. She could only bask in the feel of him, his earthy smell, and his devilish green eyes.

The dance of romance had begun, and its choreographer was not her friend or a matchmaker. It was the biology of Melissa's brain. We know that the symmetry of physiques and faces that entrance us, the moves that seduce us, and the heart-pounding passion of attraction are all hardwired into our brains' love drive by evolution. Short- and long-term "chemistry" between two people may seem accidental, but the reality is that our brains are preprogrammed to know better. They subtly but firmly steer us toward partners who can boost our odds in the sweepstakes of human reproduction.

Melissa's brain is beginning to imprint Rob. Her hormones are surging. As he tells her that he is a marketing consultant who lives in a loft in Potrero Hill and musters up the nerve to ask her to dance, her brain, faster than a supercomputer, calculates the qualities that might put him in the running as a mating partner. Already some green light is flashing that he's a good one, and *wham*, hot, knee-buckling waves of attraction and desire are flooding her body with a heady rush of dopamine—sparking euphoria and excitement. Her brain has also ordered her a shot of testosterone, the hormone that stokes sexual desire.

As Rob speaks, he is also sizing up Melissa at a closer view. If his calculations come out positive, he'll get a neurochemical jolt, too, prodding him to try to hook up with her. With their love circuits mutually revved up, the two move onto the dance floor and spend the next few hours locked in sweaty salsa rhythms. At 2:00 a.m., the music slows down and the club begins to empty. Leslie has gone home hours earlier. Standing on the corner, Melissa says that she has to go and flirtatiously turns on her high heels. "'Wait," Rob says. "I don't have your number. I want to see you again." "Google me and you'll find me," she replies, smiling and jumping into a cab. Now the chase begins.

For men and women, the initial calculations about romance are unconscious, and they're very different. In short-term couplings, for example, men are chasers and women are choosers. That's not sex stereotyping. It's our inheritance from ancestors who learned, over millions of years, how to propagate their genes. As Darwin noted, males of all species are made for wooing females, and females typically choose among their suitors. This is the brain architecture of love, engineered by the reproductive winners in evolution. Even the shapes, faces, smells, and ages of the mates we choose are influenced by patterns set millennia ago.

The truth is, we're much more predictable than we think. Over the course of our evolution as a species, our brains have learned how to spot the healthiest mates, those most likely to give us children, and those whose resources and commitment can help our offspring survive. The lessons that early men and women learned are deeply encoded in our modern brains as neurological love circuits. They are present from the moment we're born and activated at puberty by fast-acting cocktails of neurochemicals.

It's an elegant system. Our brains size up a potential partner, and if he fits our ancestral wish list, we get a jolt of chemicals that dizzy us with a rush of laser-focused attraction. Call it love or infatuation. It's the first step down an ancient pair-bonding path. The gates have opened to the courtship-mating-parenting brain program. Melissa may not have wanted to meet anyone that night, but her brain had other plans that are deep and primitive. When it saw Rob across the room, a signal went off for mating and long-term attachment, and she was lucky that his brain felt the same way. Each of them will come up against anxiety, threats, and mind-numbing joys, over which they have little control because now biology is building their future together.

Mind-Set on Mating

As Melissa struts along the city streets, sips her latte, or cruises the Internet for potential dates while she's waiting for Rob to locate her number on her website—she did tell him the name of her latest film, so if he is smart, he'll find her—it's not easy to believe that what's inside her cranium is a Stone Age brain. But that's the case, according to scientists who study the mate-attraction engineering of the human mind. We spent more than 99 percent of the millions of years it took human beings to evolve living in primitive conditions. As a result, the theory goes, our brains developed to solve the kinds of problems that those early human ancestors encountered. The most important challenge they faced was reproduction. It wasn't just a matter of having children. It was making sure those children lived long enough to propagate their genes. Early people whose mating choices produced more surviving offspring succeeded in passing their genes on. Their specific brain systems for courtship attraction were more successful. Ancestors who made the wrong reproductive moves left no imprint on the future of the species. As a result, the brain wiring of the best Stone Age reproducers became the standard-issue circuitry of modern humans. This courtship circuitry is what is commonly known as "falling in love." We may think we're a lot more sophisticated than Fred or Wilma Flintstone, but our basic mental outlook and equipment are the same.

That our mental instincts haven't changed in millions of years may explain why women, worldwide, look for the same ideal qualities in a long-term mate, according to the evolutionary psychologist David Buss. For over five years, Buss studied the mate preferences of more than ten thousand individuals in thirty-seven cultures around the world—from West Germans and Taiwanese to Mbuti Pygmies and Aleut Eskimos. He discovered that, in every culture, women are less concerned with a potential husband's visual appeal and more interested in his material resources and social status. Rob had told Melissa he was a marketing consultant—they were a dime a dozen in San Francisco, and Melissa had seen more than a few go out of business. She didn't realize that this thought was making it hard for her to figure out if Rob was Mr. Right or Mr. Right Now.

Buss's findings may be uncomfortable at a time when many females are achieving at high levels and are proud of their social and financial independence. Nevertheless, he found that, in all thirty-seven cultures, females value these qualities in a mate much more than males do, regardless of the females' own assets and earning capacity. Melissa may be an independent economic unity, but she wants her partner to provide, too. Female bowerbirds share this preference by choosing to mate with the male who has built the most beautiful nest. My husband jokes that he's like a male bowerbird, since he built a beautiful house several years before we met, and it was ready and waiting for me. Women, researchers have found, also look for mates who are, on average, at least four inches taller and three and a half years older. These female mate preferences are universal. As a result, scientists conclude, they're part of the inherited architecture of the female brain's mate-choice system—and are presumed to serve a purpose.

According to Robert Trivers, a pioneering evolutionary biologist at Rutgers University, choosing a mate based on these attributes is a savvy investment strategy. Human females have a limited number of eggs and invest far more in bearing and raising children than males do, so it pays for women to be extra careful with their "family jewels." This is why Melissa didn't jump into bed with Rob on the first night, even though the dopamine and testosterone surging through her brain's attraction circuits made him hard to resist. It's also why she kept a number of other guys on her dance card. While a man can impregnate a woman with one act of intercourse and walk away, a woman is left with nine months of pregnancy, the perils of childbirth, months of breastfeeding, and the daunting task of trying to ensure that child's survival. Female ancestors who faced these challenges alone were likely to have been less successful in propagating their genes. Though single motherhood has become fashionable among some sets of modern women, it remains to be seen how well this model will succeed. Even today, in some primitive cultures, the presence of a father triples children's survival rate. As a result, the safest bet for females is to partner long-term with males who are likely to stick around, protect them and their children, and improve their access to food, shelter, and other resources.

Melissa was smart to take her time and make sure Rob was a good catch. Her dream was a husband whom she loved, and who loved and worshiped her back. Her worst fear was a man who might be unfaithful, the way her father was to her mother. After the night at the dance club, she got a number of positive clues. Rob was taller, older, and appeared financially comfortable. In the grand, Stone Age scheme of things, he fit the bill, but it still wasn't clear whether he was the long-term type.

Chemical Attraction

If Melissa's ancient brain circuitry was scanning for assets and protection, what was Rob's brain looking for in a long-term partner? According to Buss and other scientists, something completely different. Worldwide, men prefer physically attractive wives, between ages twenty and forty, who are an average of two and a half years younger than they are. They also want potential long-term mates to have clear skin, bright eyes, full lips, shiny hair, and curvy, hourglass figures. The fact that these mate preferences hold true in every culture indicates that they're part of men's hardwired inheritance from their ancient forefathers. It wasn't just that Rob had a thing for girls with shiny curls. Melissa's hair triggered his ancient attraction wiring.

Why would these particular criteria top men's lists? From a practical perspective, all of these traits, superficial as they may seem, are strong visual markers of fertility. Whether or not men know it consciously, their brains know that female fertility offers them the biggest reproductive payoff for *their* investment. With tens of millions of sperm, men are capable of producing an almost unlimited number of offspring as long as they can find enough fertile females to have sex with. As a result, their key task is to pair up with women who are likely to be fertile and reproduce. Pairing with infertile women would be a waste of their genetic futures. So, over millions of years, male brain wiring evolved to scan women for quick visual clues to their fertility. Age, of course, is one important factor; health is another. A high activity level, youthful gait, symmetrical physical features, smooth skin, lustrous hair, and lips plumped by estrogen are easily observable signs of age, fertility, and health. So it's no wonder women are reaching for the plumping effects of collagen injections and the wrinkle smoothing of Botox.

Shape, too, is a remarkably good indicator of fertility—breast implants notwithstanding. Before puberty, males and females have very similar body shapes and waist-to-hip ratios. Once the reproductive hormones kick in, however, healthy females develop curvier shapes, with waists that are about one-third narrower than their hips. Women with that body type have more estrogen and become pregnant more easily and at a younger age than those with waists that are closer in size to their hips. A thin waist also gives an instant clue to a woman's reproductive availability, since pregnancy radically alters her silhouette. Social reputation is often a factor in male assessment, since the most reproductively successful males also need to pick women who will mate only with them. Men want to ensure their paternity but also to be able to count on a woman's mothering skills to make sure that their offspring thrive. If Melissa had immediately gone to bed with Rob or showed off to him about all the guys she had had, his Stone Age brain might have judged that she would be unfaithful or had a bad reputation. That she was affectionate on the dance floor and went home at a proper hour in a taxi showed him she was a high-quality lady with whom to mate long-term.

Calculating Potential Danger

Rob left a message on her machine, and Melissa waited a few days before calling him back. And although they had kissed on the first date, she had no plans of going to bed with him until she knew more about him. He was incredibly funny and charming, and seemed to have his life in order, but she needed to be sure on a gut level that she could trust him. The brain's anxiety circuits usually fire around strangers—her amygdala's fear circuits were still turned on full force. A natural cautiousness toward strangers is part of the brain wiring of both males and females, but women in particular give early, careful scrutiny to a man's likely level of commitment when looking for a mate.

Seduction and abandonment by males is an old ruse, going back to the beginning of our species; one study found that young college males admitted to depicting themselves as kinder, more sincere, and more trustworthy than they really are. Some anthropologists speculate that natural selection favored men who were good at deceiving women and getting them to agree to have sex. Females, as a result, had to get even better at spotting male lies and exaggerations—and the female brain is now well-adapted to this task. A study by the Stanford University psychologist Eleanor Maccoby showed, for example, that girls learn to tell the difference between reality and fairy tales or "just-pretend" play earlier than boys. By adulthood, modern females have fine-tuned their superior ability to read emotional nuance in tone of voice, eye gaze, and facial expressions.

As a result of this extra cautiousness, the typical female brain isn't as ready to admit to being overwhelmed by infatuation or the sheer excitement of sexual behavior as is the male. Women do reach the same or a higher romantic end point, but they're often slower to confess to being in love and more careful than males in the beginning weeks and months of a relationship. Male brains have a different neurological love wiring. Brain-imaging studies of women in love show more activity in many more areas, especially gut feelings, attention, and memory circuits, while men in love show more activity in high-level visual processing areas. These heightened visual connections may also explain why men tend to fall in love "at first sight" more easily than women.

Once a person is in love, the cautious, critical thinking pathways in the brain shut down. Evolution may have made these in-love brain circuits to ensure we find a mate and then focus in exclusively on that one person, according to Helen Fisher, an anthropologist at Rutgers University. Not thinking too critically about the loved one's faults would aid this process. In her study on being in love, more women than men said that their beloveds' faults don't matter much to them, and women scored higher on the test of passionate love.

The Brain in Love

Melissa and Rob were talking on the phone almost every night. Every Saturday they would meet in the park to take Rob's dog for a walk, or at Melissa's apartment to watch the dailies on her latest film. Rob was feeling stable in his job and had finally stopped talking about his former girlfriend, Ruth. This waning attachment to Ruth gave Melissa a clue that she wasn't just a rebound and that he was ready to focus in on her exclusively. She had already, involuntarily, fallen in love with him but hadn't told him yet. She began warming to his physical affection, allowing her sex drive to catch up with her love drive.

Finally, after three months, Melissa and Rob fell passionately into bed after a day lying in the sun at the park totally entranced by each other. The pair was tumbling into full-blown consummated love.

Falling in love is one of the most irrational behaviors or brain states imaginable for both men and women. The brain becomes "illogical" in the throes of new romance, literally blind to the shortcomings of the lover. It is an involuntary state. Passionately being in love or so-called infatuation-love is now a documented brain state. It shares brain circuits with states of obsession, mania, intoxication, thirst, and hunger. It is not an emotion, but it does intensify or decreases other emotions. The being-in-love circuits are primarily a motivation system, which is different from the brain's sex drive area but overlaps with it. This fevered brain activity runs on hormones and neurochemicals such as dopamine, estrogen, oxytocin, and testosterone.

The brain circuits that are activated when we are in love match those of the drug addict desperately craving the next fix. The amygdala—the brain's fear-alert system—and the anterior cingulate cortex—the brain's worrying and critical thinking system—are turned way down when the love circuits are running full blast. Much the same thing happens when people take Ecstasy: the normal wariness humans have toward strangers is switched off and the love circuits are dialed up. So romantic love is a natural Ecstasy high. The classic symptoms of early love are also similar to the initial effects of drugs such as amphetamines, cocaine, and opiates like heroin, morphine, and OxyContin. These narcotics trigger the brain's reward circuit, causing chemical releases and effects similar to those of romance. In fact, there's some truth to the notion that people can become addicted to love. Romantic partners, especially in the first six months, crave the ecstatic feeling of being together and may feel helplessly dependent on each other. Studies of passionate love show this brain state lasts for roughly six to eight months. This is such an intense state that the beloved's best interest, well-being, and survival become as important as or more important than one's own.

During this early phase of love, Melissa was intensely memorizing every detail of Rob. When she had to go to L.A. for a week to show a piece of her new film project at a conference, both struggled with the separation. This was not just some fantasy; it was the pain of neurochemical withdrawal. During times of physical separation, when touching and caressing is impossible, a deep longing, almost a hunger, for the beloved can set in. Some people don't even realize how bonded or in love they are until they feel this tugging at their heartstrings when the beloved is absent. We are used to thinking of this longing as only psychological, but it's actually physical. The brain is virtually in a drug-withdrawal state. "Absence makes the heart grow fonder," your mother would say as you were moaning in pain because *he* was away. I can remember the early days of dating my husband, when I already knew he was "the one" but he didn't yet. During a brief separation he "decided" we should get married—thank goodness for dopamine and oxytocin withdrawal. His heartstrings finally got the attention of his very self-sufficient and independent male brain, as his friends and family will tell you.

During a separation, motivation for reunion can reach a fever pitch in the brain. Rob was so desperate in the middle of the week for physical contact with Melissa that he flew down to see her for a day. Once reunion takes place, all the components of the original loving bond can be reestablished by dopamine and oxytocin. Activities such as caressing, kissing, gazing, hugging, and orgasm can replenish the chemical bond of love and trust in the brain. The oxytocin-dopamine rush once again suppresses anxiety and skepticism and reinforces the love circuits in the brain.

Mothers often warn their daughters not to get too close too soon with a new boyfriend, and this advice may be wiser than they realize. The act of hugging or cuddling releases oxytocin in the brain, especially in females, and likely produces a tendency to trust the hugger. It also increases the likelihood that you will believe everything and anything he tells you. Injecting the hormone oxytocin or dopamine into the brain of a social mammal can even induce cuddling and pair bonding behavior without the usual prerequisite romantic love and sexual behavior, especially in females. And consider a Swiss experiment in which researchers gave a nasal spray containing oxytocin to one group of "investors" and compared them with another group who got a placebo nasal spray. The investors who got oxytocin offered up twice as much money as did the group who got only the placebo. The oxytocin group was more willing to trust a stranger posing as a financial adviser—feeling more secure that their investment would pay off. This study concluded that oxytocin triggers the trust circuits in the brain.

From an experiment on hugging, we also know that oxytocin is naturally released in the brain after a twenty-second hug from a partner—sealing the bond between the huggers and triggering the brain's trust circuits. So don't let a guy hug you unless you plan to trust him. Touching, gazing, positive emotional interaction, kissing, and sexual orgasm also release oxytocin in the female brain. Such contact may just help flip the switch on the brain's romantic love circuits. Estrogen and progesterone dial up these bonding effects in the female brain, too, by increasing oxytocin and dopamine. One study has shown that on different weeks of the menstrual cycle females get more of a rewarding jolt out of their brain chemicals. These hormones then activate the brain circuits for loving, nurturing behavior while switching off the caution and aversion circuits. In other words, if high levels of oxytocin and dopamine are circulating, your judgment is toast. These hormones shut the skeptical mind down.

The drive to fall in love is always hovering in the background. Being in love, however, requires making room in your life and your brain for the beloved, actually incorporating him into your self-image via the brain's attachment and emotional memory circuits. As that process unfolds, less oxytocin and dopamine stimulation is needed to sustain the emotional bond. So spending twenty-four hours a day locked in an embrace is no longer necessary.

The basic drive for romantic attachment is hardwired in the brain. Brain development in utero, the amount of nurturing one receives in infancy, and emotional experiences all determine variations in the brain circuits for loving and trusting others. Melissa knew that her father was a philanderer, and that made her even more skeptical about falling in love and becoming attached. An individual's readiness to fall in love and then form an emotional attachment can thus be affected by the brain circuit variations caused by experience and the hormonal state of the brain. Stress in the environment can help or hinder forming an attachment. The emotional attachments and bonds we make to our early nurturing figures last a lifetime. Those early nurturing figures become part of our brain circuits via the reinforcement provided by repetitive physical and emotional caretaking experiences or their lack. Safety circuits are formed based on these experiences with nurturing, predictable, secure figures. Without those experiences, there is little or no safety circuit formation in the brain. One could still fall in love for the short term, but long-term emotional attachment may be harder to achieve and sustain.

The Mated Mind

How does the pressing reality of the "I've gotta have him every minute of the day" feeling in the brain transmute to an "Oh, hi, you again, sweetie. How's everything?" state of mind? The hormone rushes of dopamine in the brain gradually calm down. If we had an MRI scanner to view the brain changes that occur when a woman goes from a state of early romantic love to a state of long-term coupling, we'd see the reward-pleasure circuits and the throbbing hunger-craving circuits dim down, while the attachment and bonding circuits would light up to a warm yellow glow.

We know the rapturous feelings of passionate love don't last forever—and for some, the loss of intensity can be disarming. This is how I met Melissa. After she had been involved with Rob for a year, she came to see me. She explained that, for the first five months, she and Rob had had wonderful, exciting sex every day and looked forward to each minute they spent together. Now they were living together, working at demanding jobs, and starting to talk about marriage and a family. But she had begun to "feel flat" about the relationship. Her gut feelings weren't giving her that certainty anymore. It was alarming to her that she didn't have as much interest in sex. Not that she had found or even wanted someone else. It was just that now, compared especially with the first five months of their relationship, things lacked the passion and excitement she had grown to expect. What was "wrong" with her? Was Rob the right guy? Was she normal? Could she ever be happy with him long-term if the sexual spark and intense gut feelings in their relationship were gone?

Many people, like Melissa, think the loss of the romantic high of early love is a sign that a couple's relationship is going south. In reality, however, the pair may be just moving into an important, longer-term phase of the relationship, driven by additional neurological circuits. Scientists argue that the "attachment network" is a separate brain system—one that replaces the giddy intensity of romance with a more lasting sense of peace, calm, and connection. Now in addition to the exciting pleasure chemicals of the reward system, such as dopamine, the attachment and pair-bonding system regularly triggers the release of more of the bonding chemical oxytocin, keeping partners seeking the pleasure of each other's company. Those brain circuits for long-term commitment and bond maintenance become more active. When researchers at University College, London, scanned the brains of people who were in love relationships for an average of 2.3 years, they found that, rather than the dopamine-producing brain circuits of passionate love, other brain areas, such as those linked to critical judgment, lit up. Activity in the brain's attachment circuit is maintained and reinforced over the ensuing months and years by mutually pleasurable and positive experiences, all of which release oxytocin.

From a practical perspective, this shift from head-over-heels love to peaceful pair bonding makes sense. Caring for children, after all, would be close to impossible if mates continued to focus exclusively on each other. The downshift in love's mania and sexual intensity seems tailor-made to promote our genes' survival. It's not a sign of love grown cold, it's a sign of love moving into a new, more sustainable phase for the longer term, with bonds forged by two neurohormones, vasopressin and oxytocin.

Social attachment behavior is controlled by these neurohormones, made in the pituitary and the hypothalamus. The male brain uses vasopressin mostly for social bonding and parenting, whereas the female brain uses primarily oxytocin and estrogen. Men have many more receptors for vasopressin, while women have considerably more for oxytocin. To bond successfully with a romantic partner, males are thought to need both these neurohormones. Stimulated by testosterone and triggered by sexual orgasm, vasopressin boosts a male's energy, attention, and aggression. When men in love experience the effects of vasopressin, they have a laser-like focus on their beloved and actively track her in their minds' eyes, even when she isn't present.

Women, by contrast, are able to bond with a romantic partner once they experience the release of dopamine and oxytocin, triggered by touching and the giving and receiving of sexual pleasure. Perhaps keeping my feet warm isn't my husband's *primary* responsibility in bed, but cuddling to release oxytocin is. Over time, even the sight of a lover can cue a woman to release oxytocin.

The exceptional bonding power of oxytocin and vasopressin has been studied in great detail by Sue Carter in those furry little mammals called prairie voles, who form lifelong mating partnerships. Like humans, the voles are filled with physical passion when they first meet and spend two days indulging in virtually nonstop sex. But unlike in humans, the chemical changes in the voles' brains can be examined directly in the course of this frolicking. These studies show that sexual coupling releases large amounts of oxytocin in the female's brain and vasopressin in the male's. These two neurohormones in turn increase levels of dopamine—the pleasure chemical—which makes the voles love-struck only for each other. Thanks to that strong neurochemical glue, the pair is mated for life.

In both males and females, oxytocin causes relaxation, fearlessness, bonding, and contentment with each other. And to maintain its effects long-term, the brain's attachment system needs repeated, almost daily activation through oxytocin stimulated by closeness and touch. Males need to be touched two or three times more frequently than females to maintain the same level of oxytocin, according to a study by the Swedish researcher Kerstin Uvnäs-Moberg. Without frequent touch—for example, when mates are apart—the brain's dopamine and oxytocin circuits and receptors can feel starved. Couples may not realize how much they depend on each other's physical presence until they are separated for a while; the oxytocin in their brains *keeps* them coming back to each other, again and again, for pleasure, comfort, and calm. No wonder Rob flew off to L.A.

Sex, Stress, and the Female Brain

Vole studies have also highlighted attachment differences between males and females. For female prairie voles, pair bonding works best under conditions of low stress. For males, high stress works better. Researchers at the University of Maryland found that if a female prairie vole is put through a stressful situation, she won't bond with a male after she mates with him. If a male prairie vole is stressed, however, he'll quickly pair up with the first available female he finds.

In humans, too, male love circuits get an extra kick when stress levels are high. After an intense physical challenge, for instance, males will bond quickly and sexually with the first willing female they lay eyes on. This may be why military men under the stress of war often bring home brides. Women, by contrast, will rebuff advances or expressions of affection and desire when under stress. The reason may be that the stress hormone cortisol blocks oxytocin's action in the female brain, abruptly shutting off a woman's desire for sex and physical touch. For her, nine months of pregnancy followed by caring for an infant under stressful conditions makes less sense than the quick deposit of sperm does for him.

The Monogamy Gene

The love lives of different subspecies of voles also offer insights into brain mechanisms for monogamy, a trait that's shared by only 5 percent of mammals. Prairie voles are champion couplers, forming monogamous, lifelong pair bonds after their marathon copulations. Montane voles, by contrast, never settle down with a single partner. The difference, scientists have discovered, is that prairie voles have what amounts to a gene for monogamy, a tiny piece of DNA that montane voles lack. As her relationship with Rob became more serious, Melissa began to worry. Was Rob a prairie vole or a montane vole?

As far as researchers know, human males represent behaviors on a spectrum from totally polygamist to totally monogamous. Scientists speculate that different genes and hormones may account for this variability. There is a gene that codes for a particular type of vasopressin receptor in the brain. Prairie voles that carry this gene have more of the receptors in their brains than do montane voles; as a result, they're much more sensitive to the pair-bonding effects of vasopressin. When researchers injected this "missing" gene into the brains of montane voles, the normally promiscuous males instantly turned into monogamous, pair-bonded, stay-at-home dads.

Males who had a longer version of the vasopressin receptor gene showed greater monogamy and spent more time grooming and licking their pups. They also showed greater preference for their partners—even when given the chance to run off with a young, fertile, and flirtatious female. Males with the longest gene variation are the most reliable and trustworthy partners and fathers. The human gene comes in at least seventeen lengths. So the current joke among women scientists is that we should care more about the length of the vasopressin gene in our mates than about the length of anything else. Maybe someday there will be a drugstore test kit—similar to a pregnancy test—for how long this gene is, so you can be sure you're getting the best guy before you commit. Male monogamy may therefore be somewhat predetermined for each individual and passed down genetically to the next generation. It may be that devoted fathers and faithful partners are born, not made or shaped by a father's example.

Our two closest primate cousins—chimpanzees and bonobos—also have different lengths of this gene, which match their social behaviors. Chimpanzees, who have the shorter gene, live in territorially based societies controlled by males who make frequent, fatal war raids on neighboring troops. Bonobos are run by female hierarchies and seal every social interaction with a bit of sexual rubbing. They are exceptionally social and have the long version of the gene. The human version of the gene is more like the bonobo gene. It would seem that those with the longer gene are more socially responsive. For example, this gene is shorter in humans with autism—a condition of profound social deficit. Differences in partner commitment behavior may therefore be related to our individual differences in the length of this gene and in hormones.

Women, because they can have only one child every nine months, want to form faithful partnerships with men who will help raise those children. But reality is more complicated. We now know women cheat, too. Researchers have found that females of "monogamous" bird species seem to have affairs in order to land the best genes for their babies. Evolutionary scientists have long speculated that what applies to sparrows and roosters applies to human beings, too.

Breaking Up

One night Rob didn't call Melissa after he said he would. It was unlike him, and she started to freak out with worry. Was he hurt? Was he with another woman? Melissa could feel her fear physically. Strangely enough, the state of romantic love can be reignited by the threat or fear of losing one's partner—of being dumped. Being dumped actually heightens the phenomenon of passionate love in the brain circuits of both men and women. That brain region desperately, hungrily seeks the loved one. Withdrawal—as if weaning from a drug—takes over. Moments of feeling as if your very survival is threatened occur, and a state of fearful alert is triggered in the amygdala. The anterior cingulate cortex—the part of the brain that engages in worry and critical judgment—starts to generate negative thoughts about losing the beloved. In this highly motivated, attentive state, obsessive thoughts of reunion take hold. This state elicits not trust and bonding, but painful, intense searching for the beloved. Melissa became crazed with thoughts of losing Rob. The part of herself that had become merged and expanded by his opinions, interests, beliefs, hobbies, mannerisms, and character was now in acute emotional, physical, and cognitive withdrawal, deep within the reward-driven areas of the brain.

The exhilarating expansion of the self that happened rapidly during the romantic-rush stage of love is now in a painful retraction. And when women experience betrayal or loss of love, they also respond differently than men do. When love is lost, abandoned men are three to four times more likely to commit suicide. Women, by contrast, sink into depression. Jilted females can't eat, sleep, work, or concentrate; cry all the time; withdraw from social activities; and *think* about suicide. My eighteen-year-old patient Louise, for example, had been inseparable for two years from her boyfriend, Jason, until the afternoon he left for college. He suddenly ended their relationship, telling her that he wanted to be free to date other girls while he was away. Four days later, I got an urgent call from Louise's father. She had been lying on the floor wailing inconsolably, not eating or sleeping, calling for Jason and moaning that she would rather die than to be without him.

Louise was hurting—literally—from the loss of love. Until recently, we thought that phrases like "hurt feelings" and "broken heart" were simply poetic. New brain-imaging studies, however, have revealed their accuracy. Rejection, it turns out, actually hurts like physical pain because it triggers the same circuits in the brain. Brain scans of people who have just been jilted by their beloveds also show the chemical shift from the high activity of romantic love to the flat biochemistry of loss and grief. Melissa wasn't quite to this point yet. Without love's surges of dopamine, the depression-despair response descends on the brain like a black cloud. This is what happened to Louise, but not to Melissa. Rob didn't even realize that he was supposed to call her that night and had gone out to play poker with the boys. When he realized how much he had hurt Melissa, he apologized and promised always to call her. This episode made both Melissa and Rob realize how essential they had become to each other and actually motivated them to take the next step toward making their relationship permanent. They got engaged.

It may be that the "brain pain" of lost love evolved as a physical alarm to alert us to the dangers of social separation. Pain captures our attention, disrupts our behavior, and motivates us to ensure our safety and end our suffering. Given the importance for human survival of finding a mate, reproducing, and gaining food, nurturance, and protection, the pain of loss and rejection is likely hardwired in our brains so we'll avoid it—or at least move on quickly to another mate, who'll sweep us off our feet on a new, rapturous dopamine- and oxytocin-intoxicated high. What's the trigger for this high? Sex.

FOR DISCUSSION

1. Why does Brizendine insist that "the shapes, faces, smells, and ages of the mates we choose are influenced by patterns set millennia ago"? (103–104)
2. Why does Brizendine make little distinction between "love" and "infatuation" when the jolt of "laser-focused attraction" is triggered by a person seeing a potential partner? (104) Does Brizendine think there is a difference between the two?
3. According to Brizendine, what is the difference between the "love drive" and the "sex drive"? (111)
4. Why does Brizendine choose to interlace her account of male and female brain differences with the story of Rob and Melissa? Does this story enhance or detract from the scientific points she is attempting to argue?

FOR FURTHER REFLECTION

1. If "seduction and abandonment by males" is a pattern of behavior favored by natural selection, are individual men absolved of responsibility for this behavior? (109)
2. If hormones play a pivotal role in male-female relationships, as Brizendine argues, what role does free will play?

Mona Simpson (1957–) was born in Green Bay, Wisconsin, and moved to Los Angeles as a teenager. She attended the University of California, Berkeley and studied poetry. Simpson later moved to New York City, enrolled in Columbia University's MFA program, and began publishing short stories. Her first novel, *Anywhere But Here*, appeared in 1986 and chronicles the turbulent relationship between a single mother and her daughter. Simpson's other novels include *The Lost Father* (1991), *Off Keck Road* (2000), and *My Hollywood* (2010). She has won several prizes, including the Whiting Writers' Award, a Guggenheim Fellowship, and a literature award from the American Academy of Arts and Letters. She was a PEN/Faulkner Award finalist in 2001. "First Love" is taken from *Three Minutes or Less* (2000), a collection of short speeches given by well-known writers at PEN/Faulkner Foundation galas.

First Love

One night I was working on this piece and I took a walk and ran into an old boyfriend who asked me what I was doing, and I told him and he said, "Who was your first love?" And I realized, in that moment I guess, I wasn't his. So I told him the truth, which was that I was trying to write a very short fictional piece about first love and in fact this is in the voice of a young man.

I'd been in love a hundred times by the time I was twenty-five, all unrequited. What did it matter? Unrequited love lasted only slightly longer than its opposite. But I needed someone to think about in order to fall asleep at night, and so I could work as hard as I did. I promised myself if I practiced my painting long enough, work would win me love. So far work hadn't done that. It had won me a prize up at school though. I'd painted a portrait of my first wheelchair, which was thrown away long ago when I was a boy. I learned how to love by loving a thing, I wrote at the bottom in red. I was in love with Louise, but that was no problem yet. We were roommates. She kept a picture of her mailman father, the sole of one shoe three inches higher.

That night I dressed in a new jacket and the good pants. Thank God for the goddamn Gap. One thing about a wheelchair: shoes stay polished. They don't wear out. I celebrated my prize with a cappuccino before the ceremony and drank it outside on the steps. Then a woman in a suit passed fast, thighs flashing, and dropped a quarter in my cup. I was so startled I threw it at her, coffee arching through her legs, staining probably. "You little monkey!" she said. Pretty women can sometimes just change a $2.50 cappuccino.

I went into the student thing after, even though I hated this kind of party, where everyone was standing. I shoved a window open, leveraged myself up out of the chair, and sat on the ledge, the flurry of snowflakes lighting on my sweater and my hair. "I don't know if you remember me but . . ." It was Celeste, with the triangular legs. "I saw you won." She knew about the prize. I lifted the bottle to my mouth and threw my head back. I wanted her to see me out of my chair against the snow like this. I offered her the bottle and heard myself laughing for no reason. She backed away, dancing a little, hopping on one foot.

When the bottle was empty I rolled to the back bedroom, where coats were piled on a bed. My head was revolving not in a circle but in an oval. Back again every cycle passed one bad place. Then Celeste banged the door, collapsed on the bed, saying "I'm pretty wasted." She was wearing tights with a picture woven into them. She pushed her soft boots off with the fork of her striped toes.

"I remember that once you were giving me advice about moving here, and I like New York now."

"And New York likes you," she said.

I was lying on a coat and the button hurt me. My head was still revolving and I kept meaning to twist and move the coat, and then it was happening, what I'd wanted and thought about countless times, and now too soon.

"My ex-boyfriend's here. I thought it would be all right, but he's making out with somebody in the middle of the room." She kissed me and it was not what I'd imagined, but rougher. Her tongue sandpaper, like a cat's, and I worried about not knowing how. I tried to do what she did back. She was unbuttoning me, murmuring, and her hand moved on my buckle. I turned and looked outside for a moment at the stone ornaments on top of a building, the strange pure shapes of water towers. Her tights bunched at her ankles, an accordion mural, and I wanted to wait. It was going too fast, but my body flew ahead, complying without me. It was too soon and too late to master myself. Suddenly a flash of light from the door. "Oh, just my coat," the girl said. A tug, fabric scraped on my back, and then we were alone again. Celeste arched her head so I could see her neck. Beautiful. A noise left out of my chest, a long pulled rickety chain.

We were still on top of the coats. A piece of her hair was in my mouth. She sat on the edge of the bed and lifted her legs up one at a time, toes pointing, to pull up her tights again. I said, "Wait." "Shhh," she said. Then she kissed my forehead and after that she left; I felt a weight there, like a coin.

What I'd wanted to say was that she had to help me down. Now I'd have to slide, or wait for the next person. The years of my captivation I was stopped a thousand places. I waited in hallways, I waited in rooms, people said, "Just wait there, I'll be back." I became stationary. There was once, early before boundaries, when I was left out on a blanket in the sun; grass pricked through the thin wool and the buzz of the low world was balm on my skin. But I had not lived that way. I was an early crawler. Tonight I slid down using the bedspread, tossed my clothes to the chair first. But I sometimes still heard that alternate music: wheel marks on a white wall, people in attics staring out one window, beginning to love the dependence. I thought of the world outside, never Christmas, hospitals dotting the city always open and every night the same; Louise at home, probably fierce in a fit of sweeping, mad because she'd not come and now the party was over.

Years from now, Celeste will hear my name and I would hear hers, I thought. We would be part of a secret network of kindness, watching for each other's interests in silent ways. She knew, wild as I'd been on the windowsill with the bottle, that I was losing my virginity to her there on top of the coats. She had been like that, as if she were unwrapping a package.

Me and Louise that night in our beds, I always slept with my chair so I could touch it.

"Hey, what would you want if you could want one thing?" she asked.

"For years, all I've wanted was to walk. Now if I could have one thing, it wouldn't be that anymore.

"What would it be?"

"Same as you. I want to be an artist."

But that was a lie, too. An old truth that stopped being true only a few hours ago. Celeste's brisk act of curiosity and charity, proof of wildness and the variety of life to herself, had brought back a late train of a thousand memories. I loved to be touched. All I wanted now was Louise, and love.

FOR DISCUSSION

1. Why does Simpson begin the story with the anecdote about the author running into an old boyfriend and telling him she is trying to write a short fictional piece "in the voice of a young man"? (127)
2. Why does the narrator paint a portrait of his first wheelchair and write "I learned how to love by loving a thing" at the bottom of it? (127)
3. After Celeste leaves, why does the narrator describe how he has to slide off the bed using the bedspread and throw his clothes onto the wheelchair? How does the narrator feel about his "years of . . . captivation"? (129)
4. Why does having sex with Celeste make the narrator stop wanting most to be able to walk?

FOR FURTHER REFLECTION

1. Do you agree with the narrator that Celeste's having sex with him is an act of kindness?
2. Is it true that when people are young unrequited love lasts "only slightly longer than its opposite"? (127) Does this balance change with age?

Nathan Englander (1970–) was born in New York City and raised in an Orthodox Jewish family. He graduated from the State University of New York at Binghamton and received an MFA in creative writing from the University of Iowa's Writers' Workshop. Englander has published a collection of short stories, *For the Relief of Unbearable Urges* (1999), and a novel, *The Ministry of Special Cases* (2007). He has won numerous awards, including the PEN/Faulkner Malamud Award and a Pushcart Prize, and he is the recipient of a Guggenheim Fellowship. Many of his stories depict the tension between insular Orthodox Jewish communities and the secular world, reflecting Englander's own background. Commenting on his stifling, parochial upbringing, Englander has said, "When my English teacher got me started reading books, she opened the world to me. Writing became my lifeline."

For the Relief of Unbearable Urges

The beds were to be separated on nights forbidden to physical intimacy, but Chava Bayla hadn't pushed them together for many months. She flatly refused to sleep anywhere except on her menstrual bed and was, from the start, impervious to her husband's pleading.

"You are pure," Dov Binyamin said to the back of his wife, who—heightening his frustration—slept facing the wall.

"I am impure."

"This is not true, Chava Bayla. It's an impossibility. And I know myself the last time you went to the ritual bath. A woman does not have her thing—"

"Her thing?" Chava said. She laughed, as if she had caught him in a lie, and turned to face the room.

"A woman doesn't menstruate for so long without even a single week of clean days. And a wife does not for so long ignore her husband. It is Shabbos, a double mitzvah tonight—an obligation to make love."

Chava Bayla turned back again to face her wall. She tightened her arms around herself as if in an embrace.

"You are my wife!" Dov Binyamin said.

"That was God's choice, not mine. I might also have been put on this earth as a bar of soap or a kugel. Better," she said, "better it should have been one of those."

That night Dov Binyamin slept curled up on the edge of his bed—as close as he could get to his wife.

After Shabbos, Chava avoided coming into the bedroom for as long as possible. When she finally did enter and found Dov dozing in a chair by the balcony, she went to sleep fully clothed, her sheitel still on top of her head.

As he nodded forward in the chair, Dov's hat fell to the floor. He woke up, saw his wife, picked up his hat, and, brushing away the dust with his elbow, placed it on the nightstand. How beautiful she looked all curled up in her dress. Like a princess enchanted, he thought. Dov pulled the sheet off the top of his bed. He wanted to cover her, to tuck Chava in. Instead he flung the sheet into a corner. He shut off the light, untied his shoes—but did not remove them—and went to sleep on the tile floor beside his wife's bed. Using his arm for a pillow, Dov Binyamin dreamed of a lemon ice his uncle had bought him as a child and of the sound of the airplanes flying overhead at the start of the Yom Kippur War.

Dov Binyamin didn't go to work on Sunday. Folding up his tallis after prayers and fingering the embroidery of the tallis bag, he recalled the day Chava had presented it to him as a wedding gift—the same gift his father had received from his mother, and his father's father before. Dov had marveled at the workmanship, wondered how many hours she had spent with a needle in hand. Now he wondered if she would ever find him worthy of such attentions again. Zipping the prayer shawl inside, Dov Binyamin put the bag under his arm. He carried it with him out of the shul, though he had his own cubby in which to store it.

The morning was oppressively hot; a hamsin was settling over Jerusalem. Dov Binyamin was wearing his lightest caftan, but in the heat wave it felt as if it were made of the heaviest wool.

Passing a bank of phones, he considered calling work, making some excuse, or even telling the truth. "Shai," he would say, "I am a ghost in my home and wonder who will mend my tallis bag when it is worn." His phone card was in his wallet, which he had forgotten on the dresser, and what did he want to explain to Shai for, who had just come from a Shabbos with his spicy wife and a house full of children.

Dov followed Jaffa Street down to the Old City. Roaming the alleyways always helped to calm him. There was comfort in the Jerusalem stone and the walls within walls and the permanence of everything around him. He felt a kinship with history's Jerusalemites, in whose struggles he searched for answers to his own. Lately he felt closer to his biblical heroes than to the people with whom he spent his days. King David's desires were far more alive to Dov than the empty problems of Shai and the other men at the furniture store.

Weaving through the Jewish Quarter, he had intended to end up at the Wall, to say Tehillim, and, in his desperate state, to scribble a note and stuff it into a crack just like the tourists in their cardboard yarmulkes. Instead, he found himself caught up in the crush inside the Damascus Gate. An old Arab woman was crouched down behind a wooden box of cactus fruit. She peeled a sabra with a kitchen knife, allowing a small boy a sample of her product. The child ran off with his mouth open, a stray thorn stuck in his tongue.

Dov Binyamin tightened his hold on the tallis bag and pushed his way through the crowd. He walked back to Mea Shearim along the streets of East Jerusalem. Let them throw stones, he thought. Though no one did. No one even took notice of him except to step out of his way as he rushed to his rebbe's house for some advice.

• • •

Meir the Beadle was in the front room, sitting on a plastic chair at a plastic table.

"Don't you have work today?" Meir said, without looking up from the papers that he was shifting from pile to pile.

Dov Binyamin ignored the question. "Is the Rebbe in?"

"He's very busy."

Dov Binyamin went over to the kettle, poured himself a mug of hot water, and stirred in a spoonful of Nescafé. "How about you don't give me a hard time today?"

"Who's giving a hard time?" Meir said, putting down the papers and getting up from the chair. "I'm just telling you Sunday is busy after a day and a half without work." He knocked at the Rebbe's door and went in. Dov Binyamin made a blessing over his coffee, took a sip, and, being careful not to spill, lowered himself into one of the plastic chairs. The coffee cut the edge off the heat that, like Dov, sat heavy in the room.

The Rebbe leaned forward on his *shtender* and rocked back and forth as if he were about to topple.

"No, this is no good. Very bad. Not good at all." He pulled back on the lectern and held it in that position. The motion reminded Dov of his dream, of the rumbling of engines and a vase—there had been a blue glass vase—set to rocking on a shelf. "And you don't want a divorce?"

"I love her, Rebbe. She is my wife."

"And Chava Bayla?"

"She, thank God, has not even raised the subject of separation. She asks nothing of me but to be left alone. And this is where the serpent begins to swallow its tail. The more she rejects me, the more I want to be with her. And the more I want to be with her, the more intent she becomes that I stay away."

"She is testing you."

"Yes. In some way, Rebbe, Chava Bayla is giving to me a test."

Pulling at his beard, the Rebbe again put his full weight on the lectern so that the wood creaked. He spoke in a Talmudic singsong:

"Then you must find the strength to ignore Chava Bayla, until Chava Bayla should come to find you—and you must be strict with yourself. For she will not consider your virtues until she is calm in the knowledge that her choices are her own."

"But I don't have the strength. She is my wife. I miss her. And I am human, too. With human habits. It will be impossible for me not to try and touch her, to try and convince her. Rebbe, forgive me, but God created the world with a certain order to it. I suffer greatly under the urges with which I have been blessed."

"I see," said the Rebbe. "The urges have become great."

"Unbearable. And to be around someone that I feel so strongly for, to look and be unable to touch—it is like floating through heaven in a bubble of hell."

The Rebbe pulled a chair over to the bookcases that lined his walls. Climbing onto the chair, he steadied himself, then removed a volume from the top shelf. "We must relieve the pressure."

"It is a fine notion. But I fear that it's impossible."

"I'm giving you a *heter*," the Rebbe said. "A special dispensation." He went over to his desk and flipped through the book. He began to scribble on a pad of onion-skin paper.

"For what?"

"To see a prostitute."

"Excuse me, Rebbe?"

"Your marriage is at stake, is it not?"

Dov bit at his thumbnail and then rushed the hand, as if it were something shameful, into the pocket of his caftan.

"Yes," he said, a shake entering his voice. "My marriage is a withered limb at my side."

The Rebbe aimed his pencil at Dov.

"One may go to great lengths in the name of achieving peace in the home."

"But a prostitute?" Dov Binyamin asked.

"For the relief of unbearable urges," the Rebbe said. And he tore, like a doctor, the sheet of paper from the pad.

Dov Binyamin drove to Tel Aviv, the city of sin. There he was convinced he would find plenty of prostitutes. He parked his Fiat on a side street off Dizengoff and walked around town.

Though he was familiar with the city, its social aspects were foreign to him. It was the first leisurely walk he had taken in Tel Aviv and, fancying himself an anthropologist in a foreign land, he found it all quite interesting. He was usually the one under scrutiny. Busloads of American tourists scamper through Mea Shearim daily. They buy up the stores and pull tiny cameras from their hip packs, snapping pictures of real live Hasidim, like the ones from the stories their grandparents told. Next time he would say "Boo!" He laughed at the thought of it. Already he was feeling lighter. Passing a kiosk, he stopped and bought a bag of pizza-flavored Bissli. When he reached the fountain, he sat down on a bench among the aged new immigrants. They clustered together as if huddled against a biting cold wind that had followed them from their native lands. He stayed there until dark, until the crowd of new immigrants, like the bud of a flower, began to spread out, to open up, as the old folks filed down the fountain's ramps onto the city streets. They were replaced by young couples and groups of boys and girls who talked to each other from a distance but did not mix. So much like religious children, he thought. In a way we are all the same. Dov Binyamin suddenly felt overwhelmed. He was startled to find himself in Tel Aviv, already involved in the act of searching out a harlot, instead of home in his chair by the balcony, worrying over whether to take the Rebbe's advice at all.

He walked back toward his car. A lone cabdriver leaned up against the front door of his Mercedes, smoking. Dov Binyamin approached him, the heat of his feet inside his shoes becoming more oppressive with every step.

"Forgive me," Dov Binyamin said.

The cabdriver, his chest hair sticking out of the collar of his T-shirt in tufts, ground out the cigarette and opened the passenger door. "Need a ride, Rabbi?"

"I'm not a rabbi."

"And you don't need a ride?"

Dov Binyamin adjusted his hat. "No. Actually no."

The cabdriver lit another cigarette, flourishing his Zippo impressively. Dov took notice, though he was not especially impressed.

"I'm looking for a prostitute."

The cabdriver coughed and clasped a hand to his chest.

"Do I look like a prostitute?"

"No, you misunderstand." Dov Binyamin wondered if he should turn and run away. "A female prostitute."

"What's her name?"

"No name. Any name. You are a taxi driver. You must know where are such women." The taxi driver slapped the hood of his car and said, "Ha," which Dov took to be laughter. Another cab pulled up on Dov's other side.

"What's happening?" the second driver called.

"Nothing. The rabbi here wants to know where to find a friend. Thinks it's a cabdriver's responsibility to direct him."

"Do we work for the Ministry of Tourism?" the second driver asked.

"I just thought," Dov Binyamin said. His voice was high and cracking. It seemed to elicit pity in the second driver.

"There's a cash machine back on Dizengoff."

"Prostitutes at the bank?" Dov Binyamin said.

"No, not at the bank. But the service isn't free." Dov blushed under his beard. "Up by the train station in Ramat Gan—at the row of bus stops."

"All those pretty ladies aren't waiting for the bus to Haifa." This from the first driver, who again slapped the hood of his car and said, "Ha!"

The first time past, he did not stop, driving by the women at high speed and taking the curves around the cement island so that his wheels screeched and he could smell the burning rubber. Dov Binyamin slowed down, trying to maintain control of himself and the car, afraid that he had already drawn too much attention his way. The steering wheel began to vibrate in Dov's shaking hands. The Rebbe had given him permission, had instructed him. Was not the Rebbe's heter valid? This is what Dov Binyamin told his hands, but they continued to tremble in protest.

On his second time past, a woman approached the passenger door. She wore a matching shirt and pants. The outfit clung tightly, and Dov could see the full form of her body. Such immodesty! She tapped at the window. Dov Binyamin reached over to roll it down. Flustered, he knocked the gearshift, and the car lurched forward.

Applying the parking brake, he opened the window the rest of the way.

"Close your lights," she instructed him. "We don't need to be onstage out here."

"Sorry," he said, shutting off the lights. He was comforted by the error, not wanting the woman to think he was the kind of man who employed prostitutes on a regular basis.

"You interested in some action?"

"Me?"

"A shy one," she said. She leaned through the window, and Dov Binyamin looked away from her large breasts. "Is this your first time? Don't worry. I'll be gentle. I know how to treat a black hat."

Dov Binyamin felt the full weight of what he was doing. He was giving a bad name to all Hasidim. It was a sin against God's name. The urge to drive off, to race back to Jerusalem and the silence of his wife, came over Dov Binyamin. He concentrated on his dispensation.

"What would you know from black hats?" he said.

"Plenty," she said. And then, leaning in farther, "Actually, you look familiar." Dov Binyamin seized up, only to begin shaking twice as hard. He shifted into first and gave the car some gas. The prostitute barely got clear of the window.

When it seemed as if he wouldn't find a suitable match, a strong-looking young woman stepped out of the darkness.

"Good evening," he said.

She did not answer or ask any questions or smile. She opened the passenger door and sat down.

"What do you think you're doing?"

"Saving you the trouble of driving around until the sun comes up." She was American. He could hear it. But she spoke beautiful Hebrew, sweet and strong as her step. Dov Binyamin turned on his headlights and again bumped the gearshift so that the car jumped.

"Settle down there, Tiger," she said. "The hard part's over. All the rest of the work is mine."

The room was in an unlicensed hostel. It had its own entrance. There was no furniture other than a double bed and three singles. The only lamp stood next to the door.

The prostitute sat on the big bed with her legs curled underneath her. She said her name was Devorah.

"Like the prophetess," Dov Binyamin said.

"Exactly," Devorah said. "But I can only see into the immediate future."

"Still, it is a rare gift with which to have been endowed." Dov shifted his weight from foot to foot. He stood next to the large bed unable to bring himself to bend his knees.

"Not really," she said. "All my clients already know what's in store."

She was fiery, this one. And their conversation served to warm up the parts of Dov the heat wave had not touched. The desire that had been building in Dov over the many months so filled his body that he was surprised his skin did not burst from the pressure. He tossed his hat onto the opposite single, hoping to appear at ease, as sure of himself as the hairy-chested cabdriver with his cigarettes. The hat landed brim side down. Dov's muscles twitched reflexively, though he did not flip it onto its crown.

"Wouldn't you rather make your living as a prophetess?" he asked.

"Of course. Prophesying's a piece of cake. You don't have to primp all day for it. And it's much easier on the back, no wear and tear. Better for *you*, too. At least you'd leave with something in the morning." She took out one of her earrings, then, as an afterthought, put it back in. "Doesn't matter anyway. No money in it. They pay me to do everything *except* look into the future."

"I'll be the first then," he said, starting to feel almost comfortable. "Tell me what you see."

She closed her eyes and tilted her head so that her lips began to part, this in the style of those who peer into other realms. "I predict that this is the first time you've done such a thing."

"That is not a prophecy. It's a guess." Dov Binyamin cleared his throat and wiggled his toes against the tops of his shoes. "What else do you predict?"

She massaged her temples and held back a naughty grin.

"That you will, for once, get properly laid."

But this was too much for Dov Binyamin. Boiling in the heat and his shame, he motioned toward his hat.

Devorah took his hand.

"Forgive me," she said, "I didn't mean to be crude."

Her fingers were tan and thin, more delicate than Chava's. How strange it was to see strange fingers against the whiteness of his own.

"Excluding the affections of my mother, blessed be her memory, this is the first time I have been touched by a woman that is not my wife."

She released her grasp and, before he had time to step away, reached out for him again, this time more firmly, as if shaking on a deal. Devorah raised herself up and straightened a leg, displayed it for a moment, and then let it dangle over the side of the bed. Dov admired the leg, and the fingers resting against his palm.

"Why are we here together?" she asked—she was not mocking him. Devorah pulled at the hand and he sat at her side.

"To relieve my unbearable urges. So that my wife will be able to love me again."

Devorah raised her eyebrows and pursed her lips.

"You come to me for your wife's sake?"

"Yes."

"You are a very dedicated husband."

She gave him a smile that said, You won't go through with it. The smile lingered, and then he saw that it said something completely different, something irresistible. And he wondered, as a shiver ran from the trunk of his body out to the hand she held, if what they say about American women is true.

Dov walked toward the door, not to leave, but to shut off the lamp.

"One minute," Devorah said, reaching back and removing a condom from a tiny pocket—no more than a slit in the smooth black fabric of her pants. Dov Binyamin knew what it was and waved it away.

"Am I really your second?" she asked.

Dov heard more in the question than was intended. He heard a flirtation; he heard a woman who treated the act of being second as if it were special. He was sad for her—wondering if she had ever been anyone's first. He did not answer out loud, but instead nodded, affirming.

Devorah pouted as she decided, the prophylactic held between two fingers like a quarter poised at the mouth of a jukebox. Dov switched off the light and took a half step toward the bed. He stroked at the darkness, moving forward until he found her hair, soft, alive, without any of the worked-over stiffness of Chava's wigs.

"My God," he said, snatching back his hand as if he had been stung. It was too late, though. That he already knew. The hunger had flooded his whole self. His heart was swollen with it, pumping so loudly and with such strength that it overpowered whatever sense he might have had. For whom then, he wondered, was he putting on, in darkness, such a bashful show? He reached out again and stroked her hair, shaking but sure of his intent. With his other arm, the weaker arm, to which he bound every morning his tefillin, the arm closer to the violent force of his heart, he searched for her hand.

Dov found it and took hold of it, first roughly, as if desperate. Then he held it lightly, delicately, as if it were made of blown glass—a goblet from which, with ceremony, he wished to drink. Bringing it toward his mouth, he began to speak.

"It is a sin to spill seed in vain," he said, and Devorah let the condom fall at the sound of his words.

Dov Binyamin was at work on Monday and he was home as usual on Monday night. There was no desire to slip out of the apartment during the long hours when he could not sleep, no temptation, when making a delivery in Ramot, to turn the car in the direction of Tel Aviv. Dov Binyamin felt, along with a guilt that he could not shake, a sense of relief. He knew that he could never be with another woman again. And if it were possible to heap on himself all the sexual urges of the past months, if he could undo the single night with the prostitute to restore his unadulterated fidelity, he would have them tenfold. From that night of indulgence he found the strength to wait a lifetime for Chava's attentions—if that need be.

When Chava Bayla entered the dining room, Dov Binyamin would move into the kitchen. When she entered the bedroom, he would close his eyes and feign sleep. He would lie in the dark and silently love his wife. And, never coming to a conclusion, he would rethink the wisdom of the Rebbe's advice. He would picture the hairy arm of the cabdriver as he slapped the hood of his taxi. And he would chide himself. Never, never would he accuse his wife of faking impurity, for was it not the greater sin for him to pretend to be pure?

It was only a number of days from that Sunday night that Chava Bayla began to talk to her husband with affection. Soon after, she touched him on the shoulder while handing him a platter of *kasha varnishkes*. He placed it on the table and ate in silence. As she served dessert, *levelesh*, his favorite, Dov's guilt took on a physical form. What else could it be? What else but guilt would strike a man so obviously?

It began as a concentrated smoldering that flushed the whole of his body. Quickly intensifying, it left him almost feverish. He would excuse himself from meals and sneak out of bed. At work, frightened and in ever-increasing pain, he ran from customers to examine himself in the bathroom. Dov Binyamin knew he was suffering from something more than shame.

But maybe it was a trial, a test of which the Rebbe had not warned him. For as his discomfort increased, so did Chava's attentions. On her way out of the shower, she let her towel drop in front of him, stepping away from it as if she hadn't noticed, like some Victorian woman waiting for a gentleman to return her hankie with a bow. She dressed slowly, self-consciously, omitting her undergarments and looking to Dov to remind her. He ignored it all, feeling the weight of his heart—no longer pumping as if to burst, but just as large—the blood stagnant and heavy. Chava began to linger in doorways so that he would be forced to brush against her as he passed. Her passion was torturous to Dov, forced to keep his own hidden inside. Once, without any of the protocol with which they tempered their lives, she came at the subject head-on. "Are you such a small man," she said, "that you must for eternity exact revenge?" He made no answer. It was she who walked away, only to return sweeter and bolder. She became so daring, so desperate, that he wondered if he had ever known the true nature of his wife at all. But he refused, even after repeated advances, to respond to Chava Bayla in bed.

She called to him from the darkness.

"Dovey, please, come out of there. Come lie by me and we'll talk. Just talk. Come Doveleh, join me in bed."

Dov Binyamin stood in the dark in the bathroom. There was some light from the street, enough to make out the toilet and the sink. He heard every word his wife said, and each one tore at him.

He stood before the toilet, holding his penis lightly, mindful of halacha and the laws concerning proper conduct in the lavatory. Trying to relieve himself, to pass water, he suffered to no end.

When he began to urinate, the burning worsened. He looked down in the half darkness and imagined he saw flames flickering from his penis.

He recalled the words of the prostitute. For his wife's sake, he thought, as the tears welled in his eyes. This couldn't possibly be the solution the Rebbe intended. Dov was supposed to be in his wife's embrace, enjoying her caresses, and instead he would get an examination table and a doctor's probing hands.

Dov Binyamin dropped to his knees. He rested his head against the coolness of the bowl. Whatever the trial, he couldn't hear it much longer. He had by now earned, he was sure, Chava Bayla's love.

There was a noise; it startled him; it was Chava at the door trying to open it. Dov had locked himself in. The handle turned again, and then Chava spoke to him through the door's frosted-glass window.

"Tell me," she said. "Tell me: When did I lose my husband for good?"

Every word a plague.

Dov pressed the lever of the toilet, drowning out Chava Bayla's voice. He let the tears run down his face and took his penis full in his hand.

For Dov Binyamin was on fire inside.

And yet he would not be consumed.

FOR DISCUSSION

1. Why does the Rebbe give Dov Binyamin a special dispensation to see a prostitute? Why does Dov follow the Rebbe's advice?
2. Why does Chava Bayla's affection for Dov return a few days after his night with Devorah?
3. Why does Dov not respond to Chava's advances?
4. According to the story, is Dov's physical suffering a random occurrence or punishment for his night with Devorah?

FOR FURTHER REFLECTION

1. Are there circumstances in which adultery is justified?
2. In considering whether an act is immoral or sinful, should it make any difference if it is sanctioned by someone who possesses moral authority?

Comparison Questions

1. What similarities and differences are there in the responses of the men to the performers in "Helen of Troy Does Counter Dancing" and "Esta Noche"? Would Lola agree or disagree with Helen when she says, "Such hatred leaps in them, / my beery worshippers!"? (56)

2. How does clothing—wearing it and taking it off—define sexual interaction between men and women in "To His Mistress Going to Bed," "Taking Off Emily Dickinson's Clothes," "Esta Noche," and "First Love"?

3. What recommendations, if any, do you think Fay Weldon would give for preparing adolescent girls for their roles as sexual partners? How do you think her recommendations would be similar to or different from those of Joan Jacobs Brumberg?

4. In what way do the narrators in "To His Coy Mistress" and "Lust" support or contradict Louann Brizendine's explanations of how men and women respond sexually and romantically to the opposite sex?

5. How does Sigmund Freud's explanation of why women become "psychically impotent" support or deny Joan Jacobs Brumberg's argument that the "mismatch between biology and culture" imperils girls today? (28, 67)

6. In "David and Bathsheba" and "For the Relief of Unbearable Urges," how do the characters attempt to balance religious or moral responsibilities with their sexual drives? To what extent do any of them succeed in doing so?

About Shared Inquiry

Shared Inquiry™ is the effort to achieve a more thorough understanding of a text by discussing questions, responses, and insights with fellow readers. Careful listening is essential. The leader guides the discussion by asking questions about specific ideas, problems of meaning, and passages in the text, but does not seek to impose a personal interpretation on the group.

During discussion, participants consider a number of different ideas and weigh the evidence for each. Introducing ideas and then refining or abandoning them are valuable parts of the interpretive process. Participants gain experience in communicating complex ideas and in supporting, testing, and expanding their thoughts. Everyone in the group contributes to the discussion. While participants may disagree with one another, they treat one another's ideas respectfully.

This process helps participants develop an understanding of important texts and ideas, rather than merely catalog knowledge about them. The following guidelines keep conversation focused on the text and assure that all participants have a voice:

1. **Read the selection carefully before participating in the discussion.** This ensures that all participants are equally prepared to talk about the text.

2. **Support your ideas with evidence from the text.** This keeps the discussion focused on understanding the selection and enables the group to weigh textual support for different interpretations.

3. **Discuss the ideas, themes, and formal elements in the selection and try to understand them fully before exploring issues that go beyond the selection itself.** Adequate reflection on the selection and various interpretations of it will make the exploration of broader issues more productive.

4. **Listen to other participants and respond to them directly.** Shared Inquiry is about the give-and-take of ideas, the willingness to listen to others and talk with them respectfully. Directing your comments and questions to other participants in the discussion, not always to the leader, will make the discussion livelier and more dynamic.

5. **Expect the leader to only ask questions.** Effective leaders help participants develop their own ideas, with everyone gaining a new understanding in the process. When participants hang back and wait for the leader to suggest answers, the discussion tends to falter.

Acknowledgments

All possible care has been taken to trace ownership and secure permission for each selection in this anthology. The Great Books Foundation wishes to thank the following authors, publishers, and representatives for permission to reprint copyrighted material:

Degradation in Erotic Life, originally titled "Contributions to the Psychology of Love: The Most Prevalent Form of Degradation in Erotic Life," from COLLECTED PAPERS, VOLUME 4, by Sigmund Freud. Copyright © 1959 by Sigmund Freud. Reprinted by permission of Basic Books, a member of the Perseus Books Group.

Sex, from WHAT MAKES WOMEN HAPPY, by Fay Weldon. Copyright © 2006 by Fay Weldon. Reprinted by permission of Curtis Brown Group, Ltd., on behalf of Fay Weldon.

Helen of Troy Does Counter Dancing, from MORNING IN THE BURNED HOUSE, by Margaret Atwood. Copyright © 1995 by Margaret Atwood. Reprinted by permission of Houghton Mifflin Harcourt Publishing Company.

Taking Off Emily Dickinson's Clothes, from PICNIC, LIGHTNING, by Billy Collins. Copyright © 1998 by Billy Collins. Reprinted by permission of University of Pittsburgh Press.

Girl Advocacy Again, from THE BODY PROJECT, by Joan Jacobs Brumberg. Copyright © 1997 by Joan Jacobs Brumberg. Reprinted by permission of Random House, Inc.

Esta Noche, from MY ALEXANDRIA, by Mark Doty. Copyright © 1993 by Mark Doty. Reprinted by permission of the poet and the University of Illinois Press.

Lust, from LUST AND OTHER STORIES, by Susan Minot. Copyright © 1989 by Susan Minot. Reprinted by permission of Houghton Mifflin Harcourt Publishing Company.

Love and Trust, from THE FEMALE BRAIN, by Louann Brizendine. Copyright © 2006 by Louann Brizendine. Reprinted by permission of Broadway Books, an imprint of the Doubleday Broadway Publishing Group, a division of Random House, Inc.

First Love, by Mona Simpson, from THREE MINUTES OR LESS: LIFE LESSONS FROM AMERICA'S GREATEST AUTHORS, collected by the PEN/Faulkner Foundation. Copyright © 2000 by the Pen/Faulkner Foundation. Reprinted by permission of Bloomsbury USA.

For the Relief of Unbearable Urges, from FOR THE RELIEF OF UNBEARABLE URGES: STORIES, by Nathan Englander. Copyright © 1999 by Nathan Englander. Reprinted by permission of Alfred A. Knopf, a division of Random House, Inc.

life choices (sex - lust)

sex — happiness

fake - trust

love - hate -

was ——> happiness.

alternatives of happiness